HIRING

FOR

ATTITUDE

A REVOLUTIONARY
APPROACH TO RECRUITING
STAR PERFORMERS WITH
BOTH TREMENDOUS SKILLS
AND SUPERB ATTITUDE

MARK MURPHY

Mc
Graw
Hill
Education

New York   Chicago   San Francisco   Athens   London   Madrid
Mexico City   Milan   New Delhi   Singapore   Sydney   Toronto

To Andrea, Isabella, and Andrew

8 9   LCR   23 22 21

ISBN   978-1-259-86090-4
MHID   1-259-86090-6

e-ISBN   978-1259-86089-8
e-MHID   1-259-86089-2

Library of Congress Cataloging-in-Publication Data

Names: Murphy, Mark A. (Mark Andrew), author.
Title: Hiring for attitude : a revolutionary approach to recruiting and
    selecting people with both tremendous skills and superb attitude / by Mark Murphy.
Description: 2nd Edition. | New York : McGraw-Hill Education, 2016. | Revised
    edition of the author's Hiring for attitude, 2012.
Identifiers: LCCN 2016031688 (print) | LCCN 2016038284 (ebook) | ISBN
    9781259860904 (paperback : alk. paper) | ISBN 1259860906 (alk. paper) |
    ISBN 9781259860898 () | ISBN 1259860892
Subjects: LCSH: Employee selection. | Employment interviewing. |
    Employees—Attitudes. | BISAC: BUSINESS & ECONOMICS / Human Resources &
    Personnel Management.
Classification: LCC HF5549.5.S38 M87 2016 (print) | LCC HF5549.5.S38 (ebook)
    | DDC 658.3/11—dc23
LC record available at https://lccn.loc.gov/2016031688

McGraw-Hill Education books are available at special quantity discounts to use as premiums and sales promotions or for use in corporate training programs. To contact a representative, please visit the Contact Us pages at www.mhprofessional.com.

Contents

Acknowledgments

I hate to sound like a cliché, but there really are too many people to thank individually for making contributions to this book. My team of several dozen researchers and trainers, and each of our hundreds of fantastic clients, deserve a special thank-you. This book, and the research behind it, wouldn't exist without all of their efforts.

I would, however, like to highlight a few individuals who made special contributions to this particular book.

Andrea Burgio-Murphy, Ph.D., is a world-class clinical psychologist, my wife and partner through life, and my creative sounding board. Since we started dating in high school, I have learned something from her every single day. My personal and professional evolution owes everything to her.

For numerous reasons, including the continued growth at Leadership IQ, this book seemed to take me away from home more than previous books. And so my children, Isabella and Andrew, deserve a special thank-you for continually reminding me of what's really important.

I know that everything I share in this book works because I used this same hiring approach to bring together Leadership IQ's world-class staff of Hundred Percenters. While everyone at

Leadership IQ plays an important role in the company's success, for their contributions to this particular book, I'd especially like to thank company president, Lauryn Franzoni, whose strategy and vision holds great promise for the future of Leadership IQ. Lyn Adler, an exceptional writer whose assistance made it possible to distill mountains of research and interviews into this contribution to the science of hiring. Lyn has worked on all of my major books—*Hundred Percenters*, *HARD Goals*, and *Hiring for Attitude*—and I am deeply grateful for all her work, energy, insight, and dedication. Nicole Jordan, my longest-tenured executive and true Hundred Percenter, took on special assignments and filled in for me while I was immersed in the writing of this book. As always, her work was outstanding. Sarah Kersting, who keeps so many of our projects on track and delivers value to our clients, and Corey Laderberg, who really helped bring our hiring consulting services to the market.

Dennis Hoffman is an extraordinary CEO and entrepreneur whose friendship and counsel has significantly improved all of my books, including *Hiring for Attitude*. John Sheehan is a great friend and the smartest data mind I know; his insights always improve the quality of my research. And Elaine L'Esperance Cheng, Anthony Nievera, Phil Rubin, Dave Brautigan, Kevin Andrews, Ned Fitch, and Tom Silvestrini are all accomplished executives who have helped shape my thoughts on *Hiring for Attitude*.

I also need to thank some special friends and clients who exerted extra effort for this book. They are Sam Holtzman, President and CEO of LifeGift, Mitch Little, Vice President of Worldwide Sales and Applications at Microchip Technologies, Terry Byrnes, Vice President of Total Service for Caesars Entertainment, Brent Rasmussen, President North America for

CareerBuilder, ExecuNet, MOKA, the University of Washington-Tacoma, and Joe Marques and Pasquale Bisecco, University Hospitals.

Mary Glenn, Associate Publisher, Business and Finance at McGraw-Hill, deserves a very special thank-you for recognizing the need for this book and making the process fast and smooth. After working with Mary and the team at McGraw-Hill, it's clear to me why the best thinkers sign with them.

FOR MORE INFORMATION

For free downloadable resources including the latest research, discussion guides, and forms please visit www.leadershipiq.com/hiring.

Preface

It may be hard to remember back this far, but when *Hiring for Attitude* was published in 2011, much of the world was still fixated on hiring for skills. Winning the war for talent (aka finding people with scarce skills) was the dominant mindset.

Things have changed considerably since then. Just think about what kind of people companies need to succeed in today's chaotic, uncertain, fast-paced, always-on world. In addition to brains, companies need people with resilience, innovation, proactivity, determination, passion and flexibility. Those aren't things a person receives simply by virtue of having a degree or some advanced certification; they're attitudes.

It used to be that an engineer with a degree from a top school, requisite experience and some advanced certifications was considered a highly coveted candidate. That was hiring for skill and, at the time, it was thought to be enough. But with the success of *Hiring for Attitude*, a significant number of companies have seen the "attitudinal" light. They now realize that while skills are necessary, they also need to know if that engineer is narcissistic, blaming, negative, whiny, inflexible, or any number of traits that chase away other people and make this person a managerial time suck.

You've probably worked with a few of these folks, right? I know I have. It's demoralizing to work with these "Talented Terrors," people with great technical skills but lousy attitudes. They're like "emotional vampires;" they won't actually suck your blood, but the frustration of dealing with them will suck the life out of you.

Working with Talented Terrors is often so draining that it disengages your best people. I recently conducted a study that found that in 42 percent of companies, high performers are actually less engaged than low performers. This is pretty shocking because it's not how things are supposed to work. If you're a high performer, you're supposed to be engaged and fulfilled and all the rest. But when you're a high performer who's forced to work with a bunch of Talented Terrors, it's not hard to see how your engagement might drop. High performers will tell you themselves that they'd rather work short handed and pick up the slack then share their workspace with low performers.

One of the biggest contributions that *Hiring For Attitude* made was articulating that Talented Terrors are actually low performers. In the years before the book, I regularly heard these folks referred to as "high performers with bad attitudes." The implication being that skill determined whether someone was a high performer while attitude was superfluous. No more.

There was a time when you could hide employees with bad attitudes. Maybe you kept them at the far end of the hall or surrounded them with gatekeepers. You could probably even hide their salary and bonus numbers from the rest of the workforce. But it's pretty tough to keep secrets in today's world.

Back in 2011, you might actually have employees who weren't on Facebook, Twitter, LinkedIn, Instagram and all the rest. But today, those who eschew social media are fewer and further between. This means that not only are many (or most) of your employees sharing their thoughts about restaurants, sports, fashion, kids, dates and vacations, they're also disclosing about their job.

If they love their employer and their colleagues with great attitudes, their positive messaging via posts, tweets and updates could be worth millions in free branding and recruiting. One company I know asked employees to name the traits that define the organization's high performers and turned it into a word cloud. Employees are proud to share that, "we are motivated, committed, accountable, etc." via Internet memes, and by wearing t-shirts and mugs imprinted with their words. There's just no better way to recruit high performers than to have current stars do it for you.

But if employees dislike their employer and colleagues, they can scare away innumerable potential candidates. And today, those employees are sharing their bad attitude with the world. Like it or not, their attitude is directly reflecting on your company.

Not all books age well. Sometimes the world changes so much between first and second editions that any relevance is lost. But the seismic shifts of the past five years have actually made *Hiring for Attitude* more relevant. If ever there was a time when having the right attitude was critical for success, this is it. Whether you're hiring one person or one thousand, skills are good to have, but it's your employees' attitude that ultimately determines your company's fate.

Introduction

Do you remember the movie *Cast Away* starring Tom Hanks? It's about a FedEx employee who's stranded on an uninhabited island after his plane crashes in the South Pacific. Imagine that you're the Tom Hanks character, and you have to somehow survive on that uninhabited island. But instead of being alone, you get to choose three people from your company to help you survive and, hopefully, escape. Do you know whom you would choose?

Once you have decided what individuals to pick, ask yourself, "what qualities do they have that caused me to select them?" I'm guessing that you chose people with decent brains and handiness, but you probably wanted more than just raw intellect and outdoor skills. After all, being stranded on an island with a negative, whiny, change-resistant, dramatic narcissist would be absolute torture, no matter how smart or handy.

When I ask employees and leaders what qualities their island compatriots would possess, I often hear qualities like determined, persistent, calm, objective, flexible, humble, open-minded, energetic, collaborative and trustworthy. In fact, people often mention those attitudes long before they talk about the technical skills their companions would need. It's not that you wouldn't want people who know how to fish or tie knots, it's just that good skills packaged inside a terrible personality is a recipe for disaster. And that's really the point of this book.

I first decided to write *Hiring For Attitude* after conducting a study that shocked many people, myself included. My company, Leadership IQ, tracked 20,000 new hires over a three-year period. I originally just wanted to see how many new hires succeeded or failed. I didn't expect the success rates to be very good, and they weren't. Within their first 18 months, 46 percent of new hires failed (got fired, received poor performance reviews, or were written up). And as bad as that sounds, it's pretty consistent with other studies over the years.

Once this phase of the study was complete, I had an idea—what if we asked the hiring managers why those new hires failed? This sounds pretty obvious now, but at the time I couldn't find anyone else asking this question. We categorized and distilled the top five reasons why new hires failed and found these results:

1. Coachability (26%): The ability to accept and implement feedback from bosses, colleagues, customers, and others.
2. Emotional Intelligence (23%): The ability to understand and manage one's own emotions and accurately assess others' emotions.
3. Motivation (17%): Sufficient drive to achieve one's full potential and excel in the job.
4. Temperament (15%): Attitude and personality suited to the particular job and work environment.
5. Technical Competence (11%): Functional or technical skills required to do the job.

Like many, I expected that the biggest cause of new-hire failures would be technical incompetence. But the data showed very clearly that lacking technical competence is a very small part of why new hires fail; the vast majority of failures stem from attitude.

When new hires failed, 89 percent of the time it was for attitudinal reasons. In some cases they weren't coachable, or they didn't have sufficient emotional intelligence or motivation, or they just didn't sync with the organization. But whatever the particulars, having the wrong attitude is what defined the wrong person in the majority of cases.

Now, I'm not saying that skills don't matter—they do. Ceteris paribus, I will take a skilled person over an unskilled one any day of the week. But when it comes to hiring for skills vs. attitudes, all things are not equal, because skills are generally much easier to assess.

Virtually every profession has some kind of a test to assess skill. If you want to be a board-certified neurosurgeon, you have to pass a test. If you want to be a Cisco Certified Internetwork Expert (considered perhaps the toughest networking certification), you have to pass a written and a lab test. If you want to be a nurse, pharmacist, engineer, nuclear physicist, car mechanic, or whatever, there's a test to assess if you have the skills and horsepower to do so.

And even though I personally lack the skills to pass the tests for any of those jobs, I could easily proctor the exam. And if I buy the scoring key, I could grade those tests as well. And so could you. If you're looking for a Java programmer, give her a page of code with bugs and have her debug and rewrite the code. Google holds a Code Jam that they describe as "a programming competition in which professional and student programmers are asked to solve increasingly complex algorithmic challenges in a limited amount of time." Some hospitals hold competency fairs to test clinical knowledge. ("You say you know about infection control, chest tubes, and insulin protocols, so show me.") There's really no excuse for hiring somebody who lacks the skills to do the job. And that's a big reason why only 11 percent of new hires fail because of skill.

Think back to our *Cast Away* example. There are probably a bunch of folks that have the skills to help you fish, start fires, and build a raft. But what will really make them a great companion on that island is their attitude. Someone might have the technical skills to start a fire, but if they get disheartened easily, panic at the first sign of trouble, and complain incessantly, your odds of getting off that island are pretty low.

And if you have a few minutes to test people's skill, you could quickly assess whether they know how to start a fire, make a raft, spear a fish, and so on. But could you assess as easily their resilience? Or their humility, change-readiness, determination, trustworthiness, or flexibility?

This book is about Hiring For Attitude because attitude is both critical and much harder to assess than technical competence. Even in industries with demonstrable technical skills shortages, attitude still matters. People with scarce skills have the potential to be an asset to a lot of different organizations. And don't think for a minute that they aren't aware of it. This knowledge gives them the freedom to take any job they want. So the best employees are far less willing to endure coworkers with bad attitudes. Or a culture that doesn't care about hiring for attitude. Do we really think that the best people with scarce skills are going to be bought off with a one-time hiring bonus and just ignore a toxic working environment? Sure, some people will take that deal, but not the good ones. And that's why even when you face skills shortages, you still need to hire for attitude. Because you can't attract people with scarce or great skills if you don't have a culture filled with great attitudes.

And that raises another important point; if you want a culture filled with great attitudes, you need to be really selective and ensure that candidates actually have the right attitudes. Too often hiring managers will assess candidates for technical skills long before they even consider the attitudinal piece. So they discover a pool of candidates with the requisite technical skills and, like any normal person, they get excited. They've got candidates who can technically do the job. Hooray, their problems are solved! Unfortunately, once they feel this excitement, there's virtually no chance they'll reject a candidate for attitudinal reasons. Hiring managers will contort themselves like a *Cirque Du Soleil* performer trying to rationalize a candidate with good skills and a questionable attitude. 'I can coach them,' they'll say, or 'maybe I was too harsh in assessing their attitude.' Or sometimes they'll just skip assessing attitudes altogether.

And even if hiring managers don't do any of those things, there's still the problem that many interviewers so desperately want their candidates to succeed that they ask leading questions or unknowingly reveal the 'correct' answer. Let's take the question: "Tell me about a conflict with a coworker and how you resolved it." This question goes wrong with the phrase "how you resolved it." With this question, we've just signaled that we don't want to hear about any times that they did NOT resolve the conflict with a coworker. But from a hiring perspective, that's the really important information. What if they resolved a conflict one time, and failed to resolve the conflict 500 times?

By making this a leading question, we've lost all the data on the 500 episodes where they couldn't resolve a conflict.

Hiring for Attitude requires the courage to pass on technically skilled candidates. It requires a willingness to let candidates fail the interview. And most of all, it requires a disciplined and scientific approach to selecting the right talent for your unique organization.

THIS BOOK IS ABOUT ATTITUDE

This book will teach you how to select the high performers that will fit with and excel in your unique culture. It's a big departure from the traditional, and generally failed, approaches to hiring. So every step of the way, I'll share with you the science, data, and evidence to reinforce and substantiate the changes (both mental and actionable) I'm going to ask you to make.

The Attitudes That Work for Your Organization Are Unique (Chapter 1)

Your organization's culture and the attitudes required to succeed in that culture are unique. This means that the right attitudes that define a high performer will vary from culture to culture. For instance, the person who becomes a high performer at Southwest Airlines is a totally different personality from someone who becomes a high performer at The Four Seasons. Both organizations are fantastic, and they are both famous for their customer service, but they have very different environments. Southwest sings the seat belt instructions to you while The Four

Seasons serves you afternoon tea. And this fact doesn't change even within the same industry. For example, Google and Apple are both great companies that are very different with respect to culture.

So the first thing you'll learn is how to discover your organization's unique attitudes. And I bet you're going to be surprised by some of the approaches you take to gathering this information, as well as by what you learn along the way. The discoveries you make in Chapter 1 about the attitudinal factors critical to your culture will drive your selection protocols, interviews, and recruiting—giving you a talent pool full of highly skilled people with the right attitude for your organization.

Standard Interview Questions Don't Assess Attitude (Chapter 2)

Most interview questions are useless for assessing attitude, and some can even put your company at legal risk. Commonly used questions such as "Tell me about yourself" and "What are your strengths/weaknesses?" provide nothing more than canned answers. Even questions that have some potential, like behavioral questions, are often made utterly ineffective by the common practice of tacking leading words onto the end of them.

Then there are the popularly used hypothetical questions such as "What would you do if you had to make a big decision?" All these questions inspire are hypothetical responses that tell you nothing about how a person would really act when working in your organization. And finally, there is the biggest bad question category of them all, the undifferentiating questions. You're not going to believe some of these oddball pseudo-psychological questions when you hear them, unless of course you're one of the many organizations asking them.

The big problem with all these questions is that they provide zero information (or even worse, misleading information) about whether someone is going to be a future high or low performer. In Chapter 2, you'll learn about four types of common interview questions that undermine your ability to assess attitude.

A Few Simple Questions Will Reveal if Someone's Attitude Is Right for You (Chapter 3)

The only interview questions that reveal whether or not a candidate is a match for your organization are questions that target the attitudes that matter most to your organization. Chapter 3 shows you how to create these questions via a four-step strategy. You'll learn how to match your core attitudes with situations that have a proven history of revealing high and low performance. Then you'll see how to properly phrase those questions so your candidates remain unguarded and truthful in what they share about their innermost attitudes. And, notwithstanding the uniqueness of your culture, you'll also learn one universal hiring question that should be used by every organization to determine just how coachable (the number one reason new hires fail) a candidate is.

There's an Answer Key That Will Grade a 'Candidate's Attitude (Chapter 4)

What's the point of asking a question if you have no idea how to grade the answer? An interview is basically a test of how a candidate will perform in your organization, and yet, when was the last time you used an answer key to rate a candidate? Chapter 4 will show you how to survey your current employees to create an Answer Guideline that gives you the Warning Signs (poor fit with your culture) and the Positive Signals (good fit with your culture) you need to make informed hiring decisions. Once you have your Answer Guidelines, you'll wonder how you ever managed without them.

The Grammar That People Use Predicts Whether They're a Good or Bad Fit (Chapter 5)

Leadership IQ has conducted some cutting-edge textual analysis that reveals how the grammar choices people make in a job interview can reveal a wealth of knowledge about their attitude. Chapter 5 will show you how to assess points such as pronouns, tense, voice, emotions, and qualifiers to help determine a person's performance potential.

The Way Most Companies Recruit Chases Away the Best People (Chapter 6)

The talent pipelines at most organizations are filled with everyone but the right people for that organization. Chapter 6 introduces the kind of competitive thinking it takes to recruit for the right attitude, and it's more than just writing a great job post (though I'll cover that too). You need to understand the demotivators that can inspire the right people to leave where they are to come work for you instead. And you'll learn how to recruit with a level of honesty that attracts the right people while repelling the wrong.

Hiring for Attitude Will Make Your Current Employees Even Better (Chapter 7)

You want to hire for attitude, but the quest for high performance shouldn't stop there. You also want to develop more high performers from the folks you already have working in your company. This final chapter teaches a technique called Word Pictures that can be used to turn what you learned in *Hiring for Attitude* into a method for teaching attitude in orientations and onboarding and as the foundation of your performance appraisals, coaching discussions, and so much more. You'll learn the science behind what makes Word Pictures so effective and how a few really smart companies have discovered that there is a way to teach attitude.

Whether you're hiring your next hourly employee, your next CEO, or someone in between, attitude will likely be the issue that determines that new hire's success or failure. So let's get started discovering how to attract and select all those amazing people who have the right attitude to fit perfectly in your organization.

1

Discover Your Brown Shorts

We now know that attitude, not skill, defines high and low performance. But while attitudes like coachability, emotional intelligence, motivation, and temperament are all nice to have, they're far from a one-size-fits-all solution. An employee who is competitive and individualistic may be the perfect fit for a solo-hunter commission-driven sales force or a Wall Street financial firm. But put that same personality to work in a collaborative, team-loving start-up culture with a bunch of programmers all coding around one big communal desk, and that individualistic superstar is doomed to fail.

The "right" attitude is as unique as the organization to which it belongs. Just as we learned on "Sesame Street" all those years ago, we're all different, and we're all special. These unique attitudes are what make your organization so special, and that is what *Hiring for Attitude* is all about. This chapter will guide

you through a Brown Shorts Discovery so you can clearly identify and document those key attitudes. (Brown Shorts is a crazy
name, I know, but I'll explain it momentarily.) Now, you may be
tempted to say, "I know what makes my company so special,"
and jump ahead, but as the following story shows, that's a dangerous thing to do.

Jim is the vice president of nursing for a small community
hospital. He shared the following story about a hiring error
he made before he became certified in Hiring for Attitude and
learned about his Brown Shorts. When a résumé from a top
nurse (I'll call her Sue) looking to relocate from a well-known
East Coast teaching hospital landed on Jim's desk, he eagerly
scheduled an interview. Jim's initial impression of Sue was that
she was highly professional. (It was only later that he admitted
he was also thinking things like: "stiff," "formal," and "not
like the rest of our nurses.") During the interview, Sue spoke at
length of her love of analytical thinking and her eagerness to
learn the latest cutting-edge techniques. "Technical perfection,"
she said, "is always my first priority." When Jim asked Sue to
name her most admirable strength, she said, "My ability to stay
tough, even when engaged in heated and complex debates with
world-class clinicians."

Excited (and he now admits somewhat wowed) by Sue's
level of skill and experience, Jim hired her. And he did so without considering how Sue's analytical and hard-as-nails attitude
might fit in with the warm, friendly, and eager-to-serve culture
at his small community hospital. "She'd been a top performer at
her last job in every way possible," Jim said. "So I figured there
was no way I could go wrong."

Not long after Sue came on board, Jim noticed that things with his staff and the patients weren't going as well as usual. And most of the upsets were Sue related. Some of her peers saw Sue's love of "heated and complex debates" as unreasonable arguing or even arrogance, and they started coming up with excuses to avoid working with her. Others felt attacked by Sue's seemingly sharp words and responded with anger, defensiveness, and blame. Jim watched as the loyal sense of teamwork that was one of the hospital's greatest strengths began to be replaced by avoidance, taking sides, and even outright conflict. And that negativity began to register in patient complaints and surveys.

Sue didn't lack skills; she lacked the right attitude—something that's far more difficult to identify. But when he interviewed Sue, Jim had been unable to predict her lack of attitude because he didn't have his Brown Shorts (and his Brown Shorts Interview Questions and Answer Guidelines). And while he did figure it out after Sue came on board, Jim couldn't make things better, no matter how hard he tried. Even when people are willing to change (which is not the norm), it's not easy to fix attitude. Sue was used to being seen as a superstar—not as a problem. So she saw no reason, and felt no incentive, to change her attitude as Jim was coaching her to do.

Jim hired someone else's superstar without stopping to consider whether her attitude would make her a superstar in his organization's culture. "I couldn't believe how just one person with the wrong attitude could cause this much trouble," Jim said. Of course, this entire situation could easily have been avoided. Jim simply needed to identify the right attitude for his organization and then use that deeper understanding of attitude as his primary measure for hiring the right talent—a process I call "discovering your Brown Shorts."

WHAT THE HECK ARE "BROWN SHORTS"?

I know Brown Shorts is a pretty bizarre name, especially for an ostensibly serious management topic. So I'm going to define the term, tell you where it came from, and then explain what it means for you. But be forewarned. In the next few paragraphs I'm going to talk about Southwest Airlines, and I'm going to brag on them a bit (as we say down South). And no, this isn't one of those company lovefest type of books, where I spend 200 pages gushing over a few companies. Yes, Southwest is a great organization, but this just so happens to be a great story. And even though you've probably read a lot about Southwest, there's a very good chance you haven't heard this story.

Southwest Airlines understands its own winning attitude and does a great job of hiring for it. You have to fly Southwest only once to experience the organization's famous attitude of fun. The gate agents might initiate a game of "who has the biggest hole in your sock?" to make waiting for a delayed flight a bit less stressful. Or perhaps the crew sings the seat belt instructions. I even read about a Southwest pilot who walked past a gate of waiting passengers with a Dummies guide to flying poking out of his briefcase. When you fly Southwest, you notice that every employee—from executives to pilots to flight attendants—lives the core value of fun. But not all fun is alike. Southwest wants a certain kind of fun, a specific attitude, and to find that attitude. they have come up with some clever and unconventional tools to help assess whether or not a candidate has that attitude. This is where the Brown Shorts come in.

A former Southwest executive once told me a story about a group interview of potential pilots. To give a little background on pilots, you need to know that many of them are male, over 40, and ex-military. They have a fairly serious demeanor that shows in everything they do, including how they dress. So these candidates were conscientiously attired in their black suits, white shirts, black ties, black over-the-calf socks, and spit-polished black shoes. They were all ushered into a typically bland meeting room where everybody sat down and waited for the usual drill. But then the Southwest interviewer came along and said, "Welcome! And thanks for coming to Southwest Airlines! We want y'all to be comfortable today, so would anybody like to change out of their suit pants and put on these brown shorts I've got here?"

Let's pause for a second. To get the full impact of this, you have to remember that this is a job interview. You know—a hyper-formal affair in a sparse meeting room that follows a standard script where you talk about all the great things you did at your last job and why you want this new job. That's it. No getting undressed and putting on shorts, or anything crazy like that.

Understandably, a good number of the pilots were taken aback. They gave the Southwest interviewer a look that I imagine conveyed the universal unspoken question: "Are you smoking something?" I know if I'd been in that group, I'd have been thinking, "Listen, buddy, I'm all dressed up in my best black suit, white shirt, black tie, black over-the-calf dress socks, and spit-polished black shoes, and now you want me to change into some ugly brown shorts? I'm going to look like an idiot! Find some other chump to look like a fool."

Naturally, the pilots weren't that openly honest (or rude). It was, after all, an interview. The ones who declined the shorts simply said, "Thanks, but no thanks." And because Southwest is so serious about having fun, the interviewer in turn said, "Thanks, but no thanks" to the pilots who didn't don the shorts. Herb Kelleher, founder and now chairman emeritus of Southwest Airlines, wasn't kidding when he said, "If you don't have a great attitude we don't want you." The pilot could have been an instructor at Top Gun, but if the brown shorts were a no go, then that person wasn't going to fly for Southwest. (See Figure 1.1.)

Figure 1.1.   The Brown Shorts Guys

Southwest is serious about finding people who are fun. And that's not just because the organization is so nice (although it really is). Southwest also recruits for people who are fun because it helps the airline's bottom line. Fun is Southwest's competitive advantage and how the organization gains customer loyalty and ensures repeat business. Fun is also how Southwest loads planes quickly and why customers don't mind the lack of seat assignments. Reading this you may think fun is a nice add-on to smart operational management. But it is actually the secret sauce that enables Southwest to successfully execute all those operational innovations. (The other carriers know the same tricks that Southwest does, but because they don't have enough people with the right attitude, they can't successfully execute them.)

Furthermore, every employee at Southwest controls the brand marketing. Let's say the average pilot flies 75 hours per month, and that the average flight is roughly two hours long. That comes to about 38 flights per month per pilot. If a typical Boeing 737 holds about 140 passengers and flies about 75 percent full, that's about 105 passengers per flight. If you then multiply that by the roughly 38 flights each pilot flies per month, you get just under 4,000 passengers (customers) a month with whom a Southwest pilot might interact. Let me repeat that. With just my back-of-the-envelope calculations, I guesstimate that each Southwest pilot interacts with—and profoundly influences—about 4,000 customers per month. That's a whole lot of customers who could be lost if Southwest hired a pilot with a bad attitude, somebody who didn't fully represent the Southwest brand. I don't care how many billboards you rent and television spots you buy, all the marketing in the world can't help you if your employees are undermining your brand every day.

You're probably wondering about the candidates who did put on the shorts. Well, they made it to the second round of the interviewing process. You need to do more than put on shorts to work at Southwest, but it's certainly a good start that will get you in the door.

Over the years, I've talked to many Southwest executives (both current and former). And some of them had a slightly different version of this story. I've heard that the shorts weren't actually brown but rather Jams shorts—those funky, brightly colored surf shorts popular in the 1960s and 1980s. (Yes, I owned a few pair.) Apparently in one interview session every candidate walked down to the Southwest store together where they all donned the shorts. I've also talked to a bunch of pilots who said they wore the shorts or had a friend who did.

Whatever the exact truth of the brown (or multicolored) shorts, this story inspired me. And after the first time I heard it, the Brown Shorts concept began to grow in my mind. It seemed to me that every organization should have a similar test of attitude—something as simple and effective as a pair of brown shorts—by which to assess which candidates have the "right" attitude and which ones have the "wrong" attitude. Sure, Brown Shorts is a funny and weird way to describe that idea, but that's what makes the label so memorable.

I'm not suggesting that every company start asking its job applicants to drop their pants. It wouldn't work, and your lawyers (and mine) wouldn't like it. And I'm not telling you to emulate Southwest's let's-have-fun attitude. Fun may work for Southwest, but if your organization is a hospital or a nuclear power plant, fun probably isn't the key attitude you're after.

It's not Southwest's culture I want you to mimic but rather its Brown Shorts approach to hiring for attitude.

Southwest understands the attitudes that make the organization so successful, and they're dedicated to hiring only the people who truly live and breathe those core values. In 2010, Southwest received 143,143 résumés and hired 2,188 new employees. Obviously, the airline doesn't take just anybody. James Parker, one of its past CEOs, said in a *BusinessWeek* interview about Southwest's hiring practices "If you're hiring a pilot or a mechanic, a lawyer or an accountant, you want people with a high level of skill. But what we really looked for was people who had the right attitudes, who were 'other-oriented,' who were not self-absorbed, who wanted to accomplish something they could be proud of." When the interviewer intelligently asked how you can tell if someone is "other-oriented," James responded, "I always used to see if they had a sense of humor—I think that's very important."

It's easy to look at the stock market and say, "Wow, Southwest is successful." But when you examine the measures that make Southwest one of the most successful airlines in the United States, you can see its commitment to attitude at work. For instance, Southwest:

- Has consistently received the lowest ratio of complaints per passengers boarded (out of the nation's 16 largest airlines) over the 23 years the DOT has been tracking customer satisfaction
- Was ranked number two on Glass Door's U.S. 2011 list of Best Places to Work. (Southwest rated a 4.4 out

of a possible 5 compared to Facebook, who took the
number-one spot with a 4.6.)

- Has for the last 17 years been rated Number One
  among all airlines by the American Customer
  Satisfaction Index
- Was recognized as a Top Employer in G.I. Job's 2011
  list of Top Military Friendly Employers

This list barely scratches the surface of the recognitions
Southwest receives every year. You can't fail to notice that
Southwest's loyal customers (it carried 88 million passengers
in 2010) love the airline. Southwest's 35,000 employees love
working for Southwest. And it seems safe to say that the
shareholders are probably pretty enamored with the organization too.

Southwest has consistently maintained this widespread
feeling of love (LUV in Southwest lingo), and it's preserved that
love through some challenging times for airlines (like 9/11 and
subsequent huge economic downturns in the travel industry).
And the driver behind the airline's phenomenal level of success
is, without a doubt, attitude.

One final note before I tell you how to find your Brown
Shorts. Don't make the mistake of thinking attitude applies to
Southwest because it's in the service industry. Throughout this
book you'll read about organizations ranging from Google to
Pixar to the local community hospital that have discovered how
to make attitude a major competitive advantage. If attitude is a
critical component for a group like the Navy SEALs, it's probably good enough for the rest of us.

ARE BROWN SHORTS ACTUALLY SHORTS?

I shared this Southwest story because I want you to understand the origin of the Brown Shorts concept. Some organizations are serious about hiring for attitude, which drives amazing business success. But I don't want you to get the wrong idea about what your Brown Shorts should look like or how you should develop them.

I've never been a fan of business books that oversimplify things. You know, where the author leads you to believe that you can be just like Company XYZ if only you too find your magic one-word solution. Your Brown Shorts are not going to be brown, and they are not going to be shorts. And they are not going to come wrapped in a single-word package like "fun" or even "sense of humor." (Even at Southwest, Brown Shorts are a lot more detailed and comprehensive than just "fun.")

The goal is not to adopt Southwest's culture. First, your culture is unique and special. It's totally different from Southwest's, which is the way it's supposed to be. But like Southwest, you want to clearly identify the attitudes that make your organization great so you can do a better job of hiring stars who share that special attitude. Second, you're not going to get your Brown Shorts down to one word, like *fun*. Southwest summarizes its Brown Shorts with elegant simplicity, but the executives have years of detailed work, mountains of validation, and hard data about the people who will and will not succeed. The elegantly simple one-word solution for your business will come in time. But right now I'm going to show you how to get a deeper insight that will make everything else possible.

In a nutshell, your Brown Shorts are the unique attitudinal characteristics that make your company different from all others. They are a list of the key attitudes that define your best people, but they also describe the characteristics of the people who aren't making it. When you ask your candidates to "wear" your Brown Shorts, you're going to learn a lot from how they respond. If someone is happy to wear your Brown Shorts, it shows they have potential to be a high performer. More important, your Brown Shorts reveal the people you shouldn't consider hiring. And I think it's important to repeat that last concept because it trips up a lot of people. Your Brown Shorts don't just tell you whom you should hire; they also identify whom you shouldn't hire.

My company, Leadership IQ, tracked 20,000 new hires over a three-year period. We found that 46 percent of new hires failed in one way or another, 35 percent became middle performers, and only 19 percent went on to become legitimate high performers. Rounding these numbers a bit, I find that for every 10 people I hire, about 5 will fail, 3 will do OK, and 2 will be great. But now imagine you could eliminate the 5 who fail and keep the other ratios the same. So for every 10 people you hire, 6 will do OK and 4 will be great.

So if the only change you made was to avoid hiring the people who are likely to fail, you'd have twice as many high performers. Imagine the monumental successes you'd be racking up with twice as many high performers! You'd have fewer headaches without those failed hires walking around your organization. People with the wrong attitude are tough to manage; they consume tremendous amounts of management time and distract you from more value-adding activities. They also irritate and chase away a lot of high performers and contribute to a host of negative occurrences.

So while you do want to focus on attracting and hiring more high performers, I hope I'm making the case here that you also need to focus on not hiring the people who are a poor fit for your culture. The Brown Shorts Discovery begins with recognizing these poor-fit folks.

THE PEOPLE YOU SHOULDN'T HIRE

There are two basic categories of people that you shouldn't hire:

- People whose attitudes just don't fit your culture
- People who have problem attitudes

Now, there's nothing inherently problematic with the people whose attitudes just don't fit your culture. They're good people; they're just not good for you. In the dating world we'd say, "It's not you, it's me." Just because you don't want to don a pair of brown shorts doesn't mean you're a bad pilot—you're just a poor cultural fit for Southwest. Not wanting to wear brown shorts doesn't preclude you from being the best pilot ever at Delta or United or American or someplace where you're going to be a better cultural fit. Someone who's a great fit at Southwest Airlines might not be the perfect fit at The Four Seasons Hotels. Both companies are fantastic, but they serve very different customers in very different ways. Google and Apple are both cranking out great products, but they sure do it differently. A star at one company might be an uncomfortable fit somewhere else. There are no universal high performers, only the high performers who are right for your organization.

However, the other category of folks that you shouldn't hire—the ones who have issues when it comes to attitude—is a totally different story. Many organizations acknowledge only high, middle, and low performers. High performers are viewed as being desirable to hire while low performers are the people those organizations do *not* want to hire. High, middle, and low performers certainly exist, but there are actually a few different types of low performers, and some are harder to discern in an interview than others.

Think of performance as having two dimensions: skills and attitude. (You can undoubtedly come up with others, but our numerous studies show that almost all attributes of low performance ultimately get subsumed by skills or attitude.) The general rule of thumb is people who are incompetent *and* unpleasant can usually be safely classified as low performers. (They have lousy skills and bad attitudes.) These folks are pretty easily identified in the interview process and are not a giant problem for hiring managers.

But hiring isn't always that cut and dry. Some people have great attitudes but terrible skills. Others have stellar skills but bad attitudes. These examples illustrate two very different categories of performance, but both can be considered low performers. You don't want to make the mistake of hiring either of them.

Bless Their Hearts

We call the people who have great attitudes but lousy skills the Bless Their Hearts. To translate for anyone who hasn't spent much time in the Deep South, "bless your heart" is a Southern phrase that basically means "Thanks for trying, but what you just did was totally clueless. And you're lucky my code of Southern gentility prohibits me from saying anything more, because I might just slip and say something' really mean." While I currently live in the South, I grew up in the North where we instead used the phrase "God love 'em," when what we really meant was "I'm sure they meant well, but boy, that was dumb." (The expression of choice for my buddies in New York is "that poor bastard.")

Regardless of the phrase, if you're using it to describe someone in your organization or someone you're interviewing, it's time to rethink that person's performance potential. Someone with a great attitude (trying hard and genuinely wanting to please) who repeatedly fails to get the job done right (doesn't have the skills) isn't an "almost" high performer. God love 'em, but that person is a low performer, and no amount of amazing attitude is going to make up for it. And no low performer should be admitted to the elite club that is your organization.

You can root for that individual every step of the way (everyone wants to see a plucky underdog succeed), but that doesn't change the low performing facts. Sure, Southwest pilots need to be fun, and they have to want to wear the shorts. But before they can even get to that point, they actually have to show that they are excellent at skill-related tasks such as flying and landing a plane. With the tools this book provides, you'll be able to easily zero in on the Bless Their Hearts during the hiring process. As I said at the beginning of this book, compared to attitude, skills (or a lack thereof) are pretty simple to identify.

Talented Terrors

The other category of low performer is the exact opposite of the Bless Their Hearts. These folks have great skills but lousy attitudes. We call them Talented Terrors. When they're at their worst, these people are like emotional vampires. And while they won't actually suck your blood, the frustration of dealing with them will suck the life out of you.

Talented Terrors are by far the most difficult kind of low performer to detect in interviews. By definition, they're highly skilled, so lots of hiring managers get lulled into complacency during the interview because "nobody this skilled could possibly be a poor fit, right?" Talented Terrors are also very smart. They are masters at turning on and off some of their more troubling attitudinal problems. Think about the Talented Terrors you already employ. No matter how bad they're acting on a given day, if your Chairman of the Board walks by their desk, they will be full of sunshine and buttercups. "Hello, Sir, wonderful day we're having! You're looking more fit than ever. Have you lost weight? I just finished reading your letter to the shareholders, and it was brilliant as always, Sir!" Of course, as soon as the Chairman leaves, the sunshine gets replaced by dark and threatening clouds and the Talented Terrors return to biting everyone else's heads off.

Another thing that makes Talented Terrors so difficult to detect is that they usually aren't all bad. That is, they're not without some good qualities. (If they had zero redeeming qualities, they'd be quite easy to detect and dismiss.) In the real world, things are seldom totally black and white, and Talented Terrors are no different. They're (usually) not monsters; they're people who have traits that seem just fine mixed with a few traits and characteristics that will drive you so nuts that you may regret becoming a manager. See Figure 1.2 for a schematic of how all these performers and traits fit together.

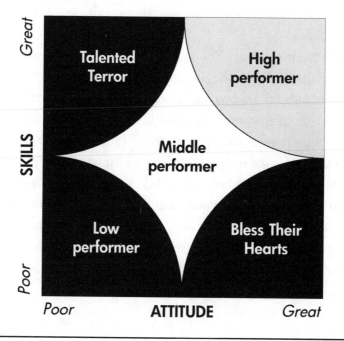

Figure 1.2. Performance Breakdown

THE FEW BROWN SHORTS CHARACTERISTICS THAT MATTER

Only a few characteristics earn someone the label "do not hire." Look at all the poor fits currently in your organization and you'll typically find that only a handful of characteristics separate them from your middle or high performers. For instance, take your Talented Terrors. I'll bet you have a few who would be high performers if only they weren't so negative, so quick to blame others, so resistant to change, so in need of personal recognition. They have plenty of desirable traits and just a few attitudinal issues (major though they may be) holding them back.

Don't get me wrong. You can't magically excise those unappealing traits and turn the Talented Terrors into the employees of your attitudinal dreams any more than you can take the Bless Their Hearts and imbue them with the skills you want. The thing to note here is that there are a limited number of characteristics that appear again and again among your poor fits. The same holds true when you think about the high performers who fit seamlessly in your culture. They're not better than your middle performers in every possible way, but there are a few important characteristics that set them apart. They might be more proactive, more team-first, more willing to look at the bigger picture, or more pragmatic.

Discovering Differential Characteristics

The key here is to think about *differential characteristics*—the attitudes that separate your high performers from your middle performers and your low performers from everybody else. You don't want a giant list of every possible characteristic under the sun; you just want the important critical predictors of employee success or failure for *your* organization.

In theory, this shouldn't be that complicated, but things sometimes get off track—such as when somebody downloads a big list of great attitudes from the Internet. She reads about all these great characteristics people should have: honesty, integrity, emotional intelligence, work ethic, positive attitude, loyalty, values, mission focus, innovation, teamwork, persuasion, effective communication, and so on. She then passes the list around to all the hiring managers and says, "Please choose the characteristics that you think are most important for our employees to have." The managers look at the list and pick everything. Seriously, if your HR department or senior executives asked you to pick from a list of important characteristics, wouldn't you choose integrity, honesty, and values? I wouldn't want to be the lone person who picks everything except those, leading to questions like "Gee, Mark is smart but is he an unethical sociopath?" And it's not as though you can leave teamwork, work ethic, or positive attitude off the list. Observe, here, that when everything is important, nothing is important.

This big list of wonderful traits everyone should have doesn't explain why people succeed or fail. Look again at the list of characteristics referenced here: integrity, honesty, values, teamwork, work ethic, and positive attitude. Not all of these are going to be equally important to your organization. For example, before I started Leadership IQ, I was an executive for another company. During a transition, I took over a division and suddenly was in charge of a bunch of managers I did not personally hire. Some were great, some were satisfactory, and a few weren't cutting it. But one manager in particular drove me nuts.

This man wasn't evil or malicious. In fact, he had integrity, honesty, values, teamwork, and work ethic. However, what he did not have was a positive attitude. I surely have a skeptical streak, but this guy made me look like Mary Poppins. He could find the gray cloud surrounding any silver lining—anything I said was immediately met with a list of reasons why it wouldn't work.

This guy didn't last very long, but that's not my point. Discovering your Brown Shorts is not about making a list of all the characteristics that sound desirable or all the traits you wish you had. This is an exercise in realism, not idealism. You need to know which characteristics predict failure in your organization, so you can avoid hiring anyone that shares those traits, and which predict success, so you can recruit and hire more folks who have those characteristics.

In the end, you will have a list of three to seven Positive Brown Shorts (characteristics that differentiate high from middle performers) and three to seven Negative Brown Shorts (characteristics that differentiate low performers from everyone else). It's this short list of key attitudes that will direct how you create your Brown Shorts Interview Questions and Answer Guidelines. First, though, you need to complete the Brown Shorts Discovery Phase and find out exactly what your Brown Shorts are.

Finding Your Brown Shorts

If we had perfect data from performance appraisals, we likely wouldn't have to dig any further to understand our Brown Shorts. If the only people who received high ratings were people with both great skills and great attitudes, we'd know exactly what they were doing and what differentiated them from everybody else. Unfortunately, attitudes are seriously underrepresented on performance reviews, and we all know plenty of people getting top reviews who didn't really deliver top performance.

If we had perfect performance appraisal data, we'd know exactly which people were struggling or failing in their jobs, why it was happening, what attitudinal problems were most prevalent, and which ones were least correctable. We'd also know whether these problems were systemic or specific to certain individuals. Again, this kind of accurate and specific data is not typically readily available. (Although, believe me, we scrub our clients' data pretty hard to glean whatever insights are lurking in there.) But don't get too disheartened because the final chapter will show you how to turn your Brown Shorts into a performance management tool called Word Pictures that will help solve these problems.

For now we need some insight into the issues I just discussed. And that requires interviews with a few of the folks who are living your culture and regularly interacting with both your high and low performers. This type of interviewing is best started at the top (the CEO if possible) and continued step-by-step deeper into the organization.

What to ask can be as simple as "In your experience, what separates our great attitude people from everyone else in the organization?" If you get a great response to that question, then you're on a roll. But you're going to find that some people struggle with these big, broad questions. It's difficult to supply a thoughtful and well-synthesized answer to such a grand question. I recommend instead starting with something much more specific, such as "Think of someone in the organization who truly represents our culture. This would be our poster child for having the right attitude for our organization. Could you tell me about a time he or she did something that exemplifies having the right attitude? It could be something big or small, but it should be something that made an impression on you."

The goal is not to be answered with generalities; you want specific nitty-gritty detail and you want it fast, so push for details. You may have to ask this question multiple times—following up each time with the question "Could you tell me about another example?"

When you've exhausted that line of questioning, start on the inverse version. Try something like "Without naming names, think of someone who works (or worked) in the organization who did not represent the culture. This would be our poster child for having the wrong attitude for this organization. Could you tell me about a time this person did something that exemplifies having the wrong attitude? It could be something big or small, but it should be something that made an impression on you."

Again, this detailed question elicits specific examples. And this is probably a good time to introduce the concept of Behavioral Specificity, which I'll refer to a number of times in this book. One of the diseases I see afflicting many organizations is what I call "fuzzy language disease." This disorder causes people to describe situations so vaguely that no one else knows what they're talking about. It's especially bad when trying to verbally distinguish between high and low performers. And when you start interviewing and surveying people to understand the differences between high and low performers, you are going to hear fuzzy language disease all over the place.

For example, imagine you're interviewing one of your executives about the differences between people who aren't meeting expectations (low performers) and those who go above and beyond meeting expectations (high performers). The executive first says that "people who meet expectations tend to treat everyone in a courteous manner." Now maybe this isn't a great example, because you know exactly what courtesy means, right? I know I do. Courtesy means that men hold open doors for women, and when sitting in a restaurant, a man always gives the woman the best view. Usually this translates to giving the woman the chair with her back to the wall so she can look out onto the rest of the restaurant while the man gallantly gazes only at her. And if the woman leaves the table for any reason, the man naturally stands up when she does. (There are days when the modern world feels overwhelming, but stick me in 18th century Vienna and I'm good to go.)

Now wait a minute—please don't tell me your definition of courtesy didn't match precisely with mine. I thought everyone defined courtesy as the thing with the chair and standing up. No? OK, let's try a different scenario. Imagine the executive says that people who meet expectations "maintain the highest standards of professionalism." This one is easy. Professionalism means that employees should always say "Thank you for your time" whenever they finish an interaction with the boss. (Think back to the television show "The West Wing" when all the lesser characters would say, "Thank you, Mr. President" whenever they left the Oval Office. Now that's professionalism.)

Oh, come on now. Don't tell me that you thought professionalism meant not showing up to work with flip-flops and nose rings while chewing gum. Do you see the problem? This fictional executive has fuzzy language disease.

Our definitions for terms like courtesy and professionalism make sense to us because *we* know exactly what *we* mean. But we're assuming that everyone else knows exactly what we mean. Go have some fun with this: pick a few coworkers and ask them to define courtesy or professionalism or another similar vague term. I'm fairly confident that you'll find their answers vary from yours in important ways.

Fuzzy language doesn't happen only in Brown Shorts interviews. Many of the items in our Mission Statements, Codes of Conduct, and Hiring Profiles also are fuzzy. Here are some examples I have collected from not-yet-fixed Hiring Profiles at real companies:

The desired candidates . . .

- Maintain the highest standards of professionalism
- Treat customers as a priority
- Regard responsibility to the patient as paramount
- Demonstrate positive attitude and behavior
- Lead by example
- Engage in open, honest, and direct conversation
- Respect and trust the talents and intentions of their fellow employees
- Challenge the company's thinking

All of these exhortations sound nice, but each is open to differing interpretations or even fundamental misinterpretation. When discovering your own Brown Shorts (and ultimately expanding them into Brown Shorts Interview Questions and Answer Guidelines), make sure you know exactly what people are talking about. But there's a catch to that. Attitudes exist in our minds, and this makes them notoriously difficult to describe. Instead of trying to come up with a verbal portrayal of the attitude, try thinking about the behavioral manifestations of the attitude. For instance, if somebody has a negative attitude, it will probably show up in the way he or she criticizes new changes in the department, interrupts customers when they're speaking, or always plays devil's advocate during brainstorming sessions.

Rather than keep this exercise in the realm of vague pseudo-psychological attitudinal descriptions, try to elicit the actual behaviors. The metaphor I give our clients is to think about painting pictures with your words. (We call this a Word Picture and, as I've already indicated, later on you'll learn how to expand this to many other applications, such as performance management.) For now, here's a quick three-part test to assess whether or not you're getting enough Behavioral Specificity in your Brown Shorts Discovery interviews:

- Is the person you're interviewing telling you the specific behaviors?
- Could two strangers have observed those behaviors?
- Could two strangers have graded those behaviors?

It's important to question whether total strangers could make sense of these interviews because, based on your familiarity with the person you're interviewing, you too might be making assumptions (you only *think* you know what the person means). Considering how total strangers could view this situation clarifies any information you might be missing.

If you find that you're getting too many vague platitudes, you'll need to do some probing. Two probes that work well in Brown Shorts Discovery interviews are:

- "Could you tell me about a specific instance?"
- "Could you tell me how you knew they were _____?"

Here's an example of how everything fits together. Let's say you're interviewing the CEO and she says, "This person just didn't represent our culture because he would never lead by example." You may presume to know what she means, but would two strangers? If not, and in this example I would say two strangers would have no idea what "lead by example" really means, you need more information. You might probe deeper by asking, "Could you tell me about a specific instance where that person didn't lead by example?" Keep asking for more specifics until you get to the place where two strangers could actually observe and grade someone based on what they now know "leading by example" means.

Most of the time that probe will get you lots of detailed information about specific behaviors. But once in a while you'll get some hemming and hawing where you hear something like "Well, you know, there are so many examples I couldn't really narrow it down to just one. . . ." Those situations call for a second probe. This is when you'll use "Could you tell me how you knew that person wasn't leading by example?" This second probe is a bit more pointed and, in a very polite and subtle way, says "I'm not going to be satisfied with some blanket assertions about their attitudes; I want to know how you came to those conclusions." The probe is friendly and respectful, but it also forces the interviewee to get his or her head in the game.

So don't be satisfied when you hear that someone's attitude doesn't fit your culture because "he's just not committed." Push for more Behavioral Specificity until you hear examples like these:

> This person arrives to most meetings late or leaves early. And then, once in the meeting, he avoids extra work, leaving it for his coworkers to do. Just last week, for example, when we were meeting about the Alpha Project, he . . .

or

> When something goes wrong, this person frequently finds another person or department to pin the blame on. Just last week, the Accounting Department became her latest target. In six months I haven't heard her take personal responsibility for a single mistake; meanwhile her colleagues take ownership every day, like yesterday when . . .

How many of these executive interviews you should do depends on the size of the organization you're analyzing. But you should try to get at least two-thirds of the senior or top executives to take part in the interview process. If you're analyzing only one division, then aim for two-thirds of the executives in that division, and so on.

Next, you can roll this process down even further into the middle and frontline management layers. Again, you want as many leadership perspectives as possible, but here, because of the increased numbers, a 50 percent sample is usually adequate.

RECORDING YOUR INTERVIEWS

As you go through these interviews, your goal should be identifying both your Positive Brown Shorts (attitudes that highlight your high performers) and your Negative Brown Shorts (attitudes that just don't fit your culture). Ideally, you want to make a short list for each.

If you want to do some advanced textual analysis with expensive statistics software like we do at Leadership IQ, go right ahead. It's more likely, however, that you'll be doing this by hand. So as you build your Brown Shorts lists, pay attention to the common themes you hear. Typically, those themes will be significantly similar concerning the people with the wrong attitudes and why their attitudes are so wrong. There will be similar themes in what you hear about the people with great attitudes and why their attitudes are so great as well. A simple tally mark (as if you were voting) will help you keep track of these repeated themes. In the end, the items with the most tally marks will be the dominant Brown Shorts issues, both positive and negative for your culture. You can download a form for recording your interviews at www.leadershipiq.com/hiring.

At this point I'd like to include a special note for small businesses and managers of single departments. You probably feel as though these methodologies were designed for larger organizations and that they may be out of reach for your smaller group. It's true that many of Leadership IQ's clients are fairly large, but we've certified interviewers from every size organization. We know these techniques work even in three-person start-ups, and you can certainly scale these techniques up or down as necessary. If your department has five people and you're going to hire one more, you won't have multiple management layers to interview. And that's fine—you can still develop your Brown Shorts. Rare is the small business owner who takes the time to sit down and review all of the hiring successes and failures. You can learn much about your culture by looking at the people who are your role models (assuming they're still with you) and the people who drove you nuts (a good barometer of someone who didn't fit your culture). The following exercise will help you get started no matter what size your company is.

3-3-3 EXERCISE

Timothy is the CEO of a small software company and one of our early certified interviewers. We happened to be chatting on the phone once and I asked him if he had ever done the 3-3-3 exercise. He hadn't, so I walked him through the process, which involves writing down (in a behaviorally specific way) the attitudinal characteristics of your 3 best and 3 worst employees over the past 3 years. Table 1.1 gives a summary of what Timothy came up with.

Table 1.1. The 3-3-3 Exercise

The Three Best Employees (Representing Positive Brown Shorts)	The Three Worst Employees (Representing Negative Brown Shorts)
Can distinguish between really big problems that could permanently damage the company and minor problems that temporarily irritate employees (but don't hurt the company or customers).	Blame others (including other departments or even customers) or make excuses when things go wrong.
Help ownership make smarter strategic decisions by proactively providing important information (including bad news) in a candid and open-minded way, without tunnel vision.	Are not collaborative, preferring to fly solo and then get all the glory, even if it means ultimately generating a suboptimal solution.
Take responsibility for, and actually accomplish, constantly growing their own skill set.	Are overwhelmed by multiple demands and become paralyzed, unable to accomplish anything, instead of effectively triaging and accomplishing all of their required work.

I've yet to meet an entrepreneur or executive whose eyes weren't opened pretty wide after doing this exercise. The 3-3-3 exercise is a very pointed way of discovering your Brown Shorts.

GETTING TO THE FRONT LINES

So far we've been getting the perspectives of the people doing the hiring. But what about the people who are on the front lines? They're typically closer to your new hires, so their perspective on who will and won't succeed is also important.

It becomes more difficult to conduct phone or in-person interviews in organizations of more than 70 people (let alone the Fortune 500 crowd). In these situations, online surveys tend to work best, but you do have to conduct them differently than you did the manager interviews. With employees, you're not asking about the people who work for them but instead those who work with them. You want to ask them about themselves and their colleagues.

You're also not starting with a blank slate as you did with the CEO and other executives. You have all the data you collected in the executive interviews, so you should have an emerging picture of your Brown Shorts. You want to obtain validation and more specifics from the folks on the front lines so you can bring your Brown Shorts picture clearly into view.

The survey for your frontline employees will consist of somewhere from 6 to 10 open-ended questions. And the best questions—the ones eliciting the most detailed responses—are the ones built around the rough draft Brown Shorts you've already developed.

Imagine that your executive interviews uncover a major attitudinal problem, something that really defines the low performers. Perhaps the problem is an unwillingness to learn new skills on the fly and, more specifically, an unwillingness to take on the personal responsibility for learning those skills. In this case, we might include a question on the employee survey such as "Please describe a situation when you were asked to do something work-related that you didn't know how to do."

Questions like this one give you specific answers to help you develop and finalize your Brown Shorts Interview Questions (and the Answer Guidelines you'll make later). You can also ask questions that will corroborate that you've understood the issue

correctly. For example, if the interviews uncover that bad attitudes generally involve reacting poorly with customers, but the
nature of the poor reactions is still unclear (or the descriptions
cannot be categorized), your question could be "Please describe
a recent mistake that you've seen other employees make in their
dealings with customers."

Questions like this will help clarify the range of issues you
deal with and, again, will help flesh out the specifics you need
to develop your Brown Shorts. Later in the book we'll delve
further into the specifics of this process, and I'll show you some
specific techniques for making the process work.

When you're finished with all the interviewing and surveying, you'll have an amazingly deep understanding of the attitudes that do and don't work in your particular culture. Almost
every time Leadership IQ delivers a Brown Shorts report to our
clients, we get feedback that sounds something like "I think
you actually understand our culture better than we do (at least
before we got the report)." It's not because we're so super fantastic smart (although I'd like to think we are), but rather because
the process itself is so revealing.

Will Employees Really Participate?

"How do I get my employees to participate in a survey?" This
valid question gets asked a lot. The answer is that every time you
give an employee survey, participation will increase as long as
you do something constructive with the feedback you got from
the last survey. "Don't ask questions you can't fix" is a critical
piece of advice I give anyone considering an employee engagement survey or almost any survey, including a Brown Shorts
survey. People are happier to get involved (whether engagement

or Brown Shorts surveys) when they know their input is going to result in a positive change.

LifeGift is an organization I'm going to talk about more later in the book. Located in Texas, LifeGift a not-for-profit organ procurement organization that recovers organs and tissue for individuals needing transplants. The organization has worked with Leadership IQ to solve many of its leadership needs, including a number of employee surveys. Sam Holtzman, President and CEO of LifeGift, is one of those rare leaders who successfully negotiates the delicate balance of running a highly successful operation while sustaining a culture that provides emotionally sensitive care and service (a pretty important attribute given the work LifeGift does).

When I asked Sam about the success he's had getting people to participate in employee surveys, he said, "Employee participation in our surveys was always good, but it's definitely increased over the last few years. We've gotten good feedback, and we've applied it to things like orientation and training and gotten great results. Our employees see the value in these surveys and that makes them eager to be part of the process—they're even willing to give demographic information. We're up to 92 percent participation at this point."

MICROCHIP TECHNOLOGY FINDS ITS OWN BROWN SHORTS

Brown Shorts Discovery can be undertaken whether your company is just dipping its toes into attitudinal hiring or is a recognized expert. Microchip Technology is in the recognized expert category, yet it is still pushing the envelope and finding new ways to improve.

Microchip Technology is a leading provider of microcontroller, analog, and Flash-IP solutions. (If you have no idea what that means, you're probably not a great candidate for the company—and believe me, I'm right there with you.) The short version is that it does microchips (the website is www.microchip .com, after all). It's a good-size company on the Forbes Global 2000, and it's growing. In fiscal year 2011 it had nearly $1.5 billion in net sales, which was up almost 57 percent from the year before. And yes, it was profitable growth, with close to 60 percent gross margins. Whew!

But all of those financial results are enabled by Microchip's culture. The CEO, Steve Sanghi, wrote a book about its meteoric rise to prominence called *Driving Excellence: How the Aggregate System Turned Microchip Technology from a Failing Company to a Market Leader.* Essentially, Microchip took everything that could influence an employee's performance and got it fully aligned. The organization clarified and shared its values, got managers to model those values, and refused to tolerate any politics, ego, or arrogance.

I know that description sounds like it came from any number of management books detailing business miracles, so let me give you an example. I mentioned the incredible year-to-year 56 percent sales growth; what I didn't mention is that the sales force is noncommissioned.

Yes, you read that right—sales engineers without traditional commissions grew sales 56 percent in 2011 at a billion-dollar company. They have bonuses tied to worldwide sales goals, but not the individual incentives you'd typically see. And Microchip has unbelievably low turnover in its sales force (low single digit percentage).

Microchip accomplished all this because it hires for attitude. It finds people who fit its highly collaborative and ego-free—yet still hyper-technical—culture. But the folks at Microchip are high performers who aren't easily satisfied. It needs more salespeople to continue driving growth, and it wants turnover, as low as it already is, cut in half. So Mitch Little, Vice President of Worldwide Sales and Applications, attended one of Leadership IQ's webinars on Hiring for Attitude and immediately thereafter we launched a Brown Shorts project.

Mitch Little is a brilliant guy—you can see the results he's gotten as head of sales. And he's won awards (like his Stevie Award that the *New York Post* called "the business world's own Oscars") for building an incredible and noncommissioned sales organization. But despite Microchip's accomplishments, Mitch wanted to fine-tune the company and push further.

Some of Microchip's Brown Shorts were obvious just from reading the book and reviewing the organization's awards. But as we began the Brown Shorts Discovery, we learned that there were additional factors driving the company's success. For example, one of the big Brown Shorts we uncovered was that the most successful sales engineers had tremendously high empathy for both customers and colleagues. And when we probed for more information about the behaviors that define empathy at Microchip (so two strangers could observe and grade it), we learned the following:

A poor fit in the Microchip culture would deal with frustrated (and frustrating) customers by:

- Condescending ("I'm the expert in our products, you're not, so . . .")
- Placating ("Here, have some free software and stop complaining . . .")

- Overwhelming ("You want technical specifications? Well, open the warehouse, because I've got a truckload of technical specifications . . .")
- Challenging ("That last request you made is technically infeasible—tell me how you even arrived at those calculations .")
- Ignoring ("That customer has a crazy request every time he's anxious, but ignore it for a day and he'll settle down and forget about it .")

In contrast, potential high performers not only avoided all those bad behaviors, but also exhibited:

- Understanding ("A customer got really angry and swore at me up and down. But I knew she was just stressed and reacting in the moment, and I was sympathetic to her plight of being caught between multiple bosses' requests.")
- Caring ("Even our best friends sometimes get quarrelsome and difficult, but we don't abandon them or refuse to help. In fact, when a friend is in trouble, it usually makes us want to get in there and help even more.")
- Persistence ("I ended up staying on the phone with her until almost midnight, but we finally got things figured out and working right.")
- Objectivity ("When I felt myself getting defensive, I took a mental step back to get an objective take on how the customer viewed the situation.")
- Sincerity ("I suggested the wrong product to a customer so he abruptly decided to stop doing business with us. I

called a meeting with their management and apologized with no excuses. They're now back with us.")

The more we uncovered Microchip's Brown Shorts—the secret drivers of success that not even the organization had fully recognized—the clearer it became that we could spot future high and low performers a mile away. Of course, after this phase we turned those characteristics into Brown Shorts Interview Questions and Answer Guidelines. But the whole process (for Microchip or anybody else) rests on understanding those key differentiators that drive your success and separate you from everybody else. We uncovered more Brown Shorts characteristics, but I don't want to divulge all Microchip's secrets.

Microchip's culture isn't for everybody—in fact, it scares away some people (people who wouldn't fit in anyway). But the organization's financial results are strong evidence that this is a culture that works incredibly well. And as great as Microchip currently is, they kept digging and further clarifying to reveal the select attitudinal factors that define organizational success. Mitch tells me the whole process is going to cut turnover in half. And given what I've seen from Microchip so far, he has me convinced.

For free downloadable resources including the latest research, discussion guides, and forms please visit www.leadershipiq.com/hiring.

2

The Interview Questions
You Shouldn't Be Asking

Now that you've discovered your Brown Shorts, you're almost ready to turn those insights into powerful Brown Shorts Interview Questions. But before you do, you want to make sure you have enough time during the interview to ask those great questions. The most effective way to use your time more efficiently is to eliminate the bad questions you (and a lot of others) are currently asking.

Many interview questions are utterly useless, and some are actually dangerous (legally speaking). And many commonly asked questions have a built-in flaw whereby they elicit rehearsed replies. As a result, they deliver skewed data that can negatively impact your hiring decisions.

This chapter introduces four types of bad interview questions. There are a lot more than that, but I selected these four categories because they represent the kinds of poorly formed interview questions that Leadership IQ surveys and studies have found to be the most commonly used across a broad spectrum of industries. If you (or your organization) currently use any of these types of questions, it's important to understand why they are so bad and to stop using them immediately. Remember that this is not a comprehensive list of bad interview questions. Even if you don't recognize any of these questions as the type you ask, it's still critical to analyze those questions you do use and ask yourself "Is this question helping or hurting my quest to Hire for Attitude?" If you find you have questions that do nothing to help you Hire for Attitude, get rid of them to make room for your Brown Shorts Interview Questions.

DON'T ASK THESE QUESTIONS NUMBER 1: THE THREE MOST COMMON QUESTIONS

Leadership IQ's numerous studies and interviews with hiring managers have revealed that the following three questions are the ones most interviewers use. Frighteningly, these bad questions are the ones a lot of interviewers rely upon when making their final hiring decisions.

- Tell me about yourself.
- What are your strengths?
- What are your weaknesses?

These are bad questions for a variety of reasons. First, these questions are too vague; they allow for only vacuous answers.

Second, because these questions are so well known, and because it's remarkably easy to conceive of and verbalize any number of empty answers, virtually every candidate has ready a canned answer. And third, because all those rehearsed vacuous answers sound the same, it's nearly impossible to differentiate between future high and low performers based on any of the answers.

Some people try to justify their use of these questions by arguing that the vagueness of the questions and the vacuous nature of the answers they inspire make them a rapport-building exercise to be used at the beginning of the interview. But rapport-building is all about getting people relaxed and making them feel comfortable enough to open up to you, not making them recite a vapid answer to a question that is trying to judge them.

Clearly, you want to learn about the strengths and weaknesses of people you interview, but asking these three questions will only reveal how well your candidate can recite scripted answers. The purpose of an interview isn't to test recitation skills, but rather to accurately reveal how a person will perform when working for you. To further prove that the questions "tell me about yourself," "what are your strengths?" and "what are your weaknesses?" are worthless, think about the answers you usually get when you ask an applicant a question such as "So tell me about yourself . . ."

The typical response goes something like this: "Well, I'm a motivated self-starter—always have been. Ever since I was a kid I've really loved hard work. Those were the values I grew up with: working hard, but not in a way that burns out the people around me; persevering, but still knowing when enough is enough; and collaborating but also helping other people get better. I've also been told that I have a lot of humility and a real appreciation for the feelings of others. I guess some people would call that emotional intelligence. In conclusion, I'm really dedicated to bringing value to others, especially my boss. I've never desired a work-life balance for myself (due to some "gifted child" experiments when I was a kid, I don't need sleep). But I am 100 percent dedicated to being good in my job so that my boss can achieve an amazing work-life balance."

Wouldn't it be wonderful if all this were true? Honestly, though, what can you really learn from this response? The only thing I learned is that this potential employee is a good script writer who has a talent for reciting lines. And if line recitation happens to be a critical characteristic for the job, then perhaps you should consider this candidate. Beyond that, there's not much else to be learned from this response or any responses like it.

Now imagine that after you shake off your amazement at your candidate's brilliant example of critical self-reflection (please note the sarcasm), you ask a follow-up question. "Wow, that all sounds really great. I don't suppose you have any weaknesses, do you?"

Given the candidate's initial response, it shouldn't be difficult to predict the kind of answer this follow up will elicit: "I was really hoping you wouldn't ask me that because I never lie, and I actually do have two weaknesses. First, I have been told by my previous bosses that I work too hard. I get way too involved with my work and I end up giving too much of myself to the job. This also feeds my perfectionist streak; I really like to make sure that my boss never ever sees a mistake come from me. And this leads to my second weakness, which is that sometimes I care too much about my teammates. Here again, I'm guilty of giving way too much of myself in my efforts to help them achieve greatness."

Now, if reports started rolling in that interviewers were asking "What are your weaknesses?" and hearing responses such as "I have a violent temper and I stalked my last boss," or "I hate people, and I can't stand taking orders," then perhaps this line of questioning would be valuable. But honest responses such as these are rarely heard in an interview, and the odds are small that anyone will answer any of these three questions with complete honesty.

One of the most fundamental tests of the effectiveness of an interview question is the extent to which it helps differentiate between high and low performers. Any interview question that doesn't distinguish between these two groups is the equivalent of giving a college exam on which every student automatically scores an A. What's the point of giving a test where everyone gets the same grade? Beware of both any response that comes off sounding puffed-up and hollow and any question that produces hollow answers.

DON'T ASK THESE QUESTIONS NUMBER 2: THE BEHAVIORAL QUESTIONS

You're probably familiar with the concept of a behavioral interview question. It's essentially a question based on the philosophy that how a person responded to a past situation accurately predicts how that person will respond when that situation occurs again. These questions typically begin with the phrase "Tell me about a time . . ."

The following are some standard behavioral interview questions commonly asked by managers around the globe, and every one of them is seriously flawed. See if you can identify the problem.

- Tell me about a time when you had to adapt to a difficult situation. What did you do?
- Tell me about a time when you had to balance competing priorities and did so successfully.
- Tell me about a conflict with a coworker and how you resolved it.

There is nothing inherently wrong with hiring questions that target previous behaviors. Past behavior can be a great predictor of future behavior. But there's a caveat. Behavioral questions are only effective when they prompt a response that reveals the truth about both weaknesses and strengths. And that's where these three questions go horribly wrong. Every one of them contains an obvious tip-off on how to game a response that showcases the good and hides the bad. They are all leading questions—they lead the candidate to give the desired answer.

Imagine you have a highly collaborative culture that includes lots of teamwork and shared decision making, and you want to assess which job candidates are a good fit. So, in your next interview, you ask a question such as "Listen, our corporate culture is highly collaborative and really based around teamwork. So tell me about your teamwork skills."

That question is about as leading as a question gets. The candidate would have to be completely clueless not to deliver a solid answer. You just revealed that you value teamwork and then asked him to concur with your stated love of teamwork by providing some easy-to-generate examples.

It's fairly easy to see the flaws in this teamwork question—how it leads the candidate to figure out the correct answer. But the three examples of behavioral questions that I began this section with, while more subtle, are just as problematic.

Despite the variety of personalities and attitudes out there, you can still roughly categorize people into two groups: the problem bringers and problem solvers. When you ask a problem bringer about a problem, you'll hear about the problem and nothing more. We've all worked with these folks, and you know that they can spend all day telling you about a problem without ever coming close to offering a solution. By contrast, when you ask a problem solver about a problem, you'll hear about the problem, but you'll also hear some potential solutions. That's because problem solvers can't even think of a problem without instantly generating possible solutions. For them, separating problems and solutions is as ludicrous as separating wet from water. And no matter what particular attitude you're looking to hire, you'll want that person to have a problem solver predisposition.

Leading questions rob you of your chance to find out if someone is a problem bringer or a problem solver. Let's say you ask a candidate a typical behavioral question, something like "Tell me about a time when you had to adapt to a difficult situation." It may sound like a good question, but the word *adapt* turns it into a leading question, sending a clear signal that you want to hear only about a time the candidate adapted (instead of the many times that person failed to adapt). Now, in the case of true high performer candidates (the problem solvers), this isn't such a big deal. These folks have plenty of examples that describe a time they successfully adapted to a difficult situation. And even if you lose the leading part of that question, a high performer is going to tell you not only about the difficult situation, but also about the steps taken to adapt to that difficult situation. As I've said, it's practically impossible for high performers to imagine facing a difficult situation without also successfully adapting to it.

But for problem bringers (low performers), using the word *adapted* renders this question useless. The problem bringers have probably faced countless difficult situations, but it's unlikely that they successfully adapted to any of them. In fact, the times problem bringers successfully adapted probably constitute such a tiny fraction of the times they faced difficult situations that it would never even occur to them to search their mental databases and find the one instance where it happened. When you introduce a leading question, you're not giving the problem bringers the chance to disclose that information. However, cut out the leading part and ask only about facing a difficult situation and all those problem bringer personalities are going to tell you the truth. They'll tell you about a time they faced a difficult situation, but they aren't going to offer up any information about how they solved the problem. You asked about a problem, and that's what you're going to hear about (and just think how much fun that personality type would be to work with).

Now consider the question "Tell me about a conflict with a coworker and how you resolved it." I bet you picked right up on the leading part that asks about a resolution. At this point you should recognize the signal it sends: forget about all the times you did *not* resolve the conflict with a coworker and just tell me about a time you did. But from a hiring perspective, that information you just told the candidate to dismiss is what's important to know. What if the candidate resolved the conflict once and failed to resolve it 500 times? By making this a leading question, you've lost all the data on the 500 episodes when there was no resolve.

Or how about the question "Tell me about a time when you had to balance competing priorities and did so successfully." "Balance competing priorities" aided by "successfully" clues the candidate to *not* tell you about all the times he struggled or failed to balance competing priorities (good information to have). Instead, he is going to search his memory to find the one time he was able to balance priorities successfully and use that as his example.

Interview questions, and especially the behavioral ones, go wrong when they become leading questions. When we explicitly or implicitly signal to our candidates what answer we're looking for, it stops them from revealing their true sentiments. There are many interview questions where that kind of signaling is obvious. In fact, when Leadership IQ is called in to evaluate an organization's interview questions, we usually find that at least two-thirds of the behavioral questions being asked are leading.

Of course, the big questions are Will people be honest when you strip out the leading parts of a question? Will they actually reveal the truth about whether they are problem solvers or problem bringers? Leadership IQ's data say yes. In a recent project we redesigned a client's leading interview questions. One of the revamped questions asked "Tell me about a time you lacked the

skills or knowledge to complete an assignment." (They removed
the leading "and tell me what you did.") Here are snippets of
some actual answers:

- "Happened all the time; that's why I'm interviewing
  with you guys."
- "I told them to find somebody else."
- "That's why we have customer service; let them figure it
  out."
- "When I don't know what to do, I'd rather do nothing
  at all."
- "I just ignored their request."

Those were the problem bringers. Here are a few examples of
answers the revamped, nonleading question elicited from the
problem solvers:

- "I wasn't afraid to admit that I lacked the skills I needed
  and was easily able to find a peer who caught me up to
  speed."
- "I enlisted the help of someone from corporate who
  was familiar with the tool I did not know how to use.
  I didn't have to solve the problem from scratch, and it
  sure felt good to share the credit for a job well done."
- "I made certain to stay in close communication with the
  customer. They were aware that I didn't have a ready
  solution, but I made sure they knew that I was doing all
  I could to get them the information they needed. As a
  result, we not only held on to one of our best customers,

we also gained their appreciation regarding the extent to which our organization will go to deliver great customer service."

Obviously, the problem-bringer answers are terrible and the problem-solver answers are great. But these are all honest answers, and because they are honest, any interviewer could easily use the information to make an accurate assessment about attitude. This, then, is the whole point of an interview question—to reveal the candidate's true attitude, not his or her canned, rehearsed interview personality.

DON'T ASK THESE QUESTIONS NUMBER 3: THE HYPOTHETICAL QUESTIONS

Most hypothetical questions begin by asking "What would you do if . . ." followed by some kind of situation such as "you had to make a big decision?" Hypothetical questions are problematic because the answers they inspire are usually idealized. You'll probably get a lot of responses that sound like something a high performer would do, but those answers will rarely reflect reality. Despite what we each might like to believe about ourselves, there's a huge gap between our hypothetical selves and our real selves.

For instance, let's say I selected some random people off the street and asked "What would you do if you saw a complete stranger being assaulted in a public place?" I can guarantee that virtually every person I asked would give one of two possible answers: "I'd rush right in to help" or "I'd immediately call 911." Isn't that how you would respond?

Both responses sound great, like true high performers. These responses, though, are nothing more than conjecture, a notion or supposition of what those people think they would do in that situation. However, put those same folks in the real-life position of witnessing a public assault, and there's no telling what they might do. Some of them might actually freeze with fear. Or maybe, in an effort to protect their lives, others would run away from the scene and then call the police. The bottom line is that it's dangerous to try and predict what people will do in reality by asking them about a hypothetical situation.

There was a news story a while back about a Kansas woman who was stabbed during the robbery of a convenience store. The entire incident was caught on the store's surveillance cameras. The stabbing was brutal, but that's not why the story made national headlines. Footage from the camera showed five patrons stepping over the woman's prone and bleeding body to exit; not one of them stopped or did anything to help. One of them even paused to take a picture of her with a cell phone. It was only after all the witnesses had left the store that someone called the police. The woman later died at the hospital.

There were numerous online comments made in response to this event, and a lot of them included statements of public outrage—things like "I'd never have walked away." And yet, all five people in that store that day showed no hesitation in stepping over a dying woman to exit a bad situation. Maybe if at least one of them had stayed behind to help or to call 911, I'd have more faith in hypothetical responses. But they didn't, and so I don't, and neither should you.

Another problem with most hypothetical questions is that it's not difficult to discern what the interviewer wants in response, and thus it's easy to come up with the correct answer. For example, take the popular hypothetical interview question "How would you deal with personality clashes among team members?" There are lots of different ways to answer this question, all of which sound intelligent. And they are all responses that would likely be successful—if they were implemented the way they were stated.

For instance, if I were asked the personality clash question, I'd probably shape my answer something like this: "I've found that there can be four different root causes of personality clashes among team members, and each one requires a different response. First, there can be clashes when the team doesn't have a clearly articulated goal that collectively binds and bonds the group. So, this kind of situation requires some work to align the group with a collective strategy. Second, there might be a long and troubled history between two or more members. In this case, I'd take a different approach," and so on.

My answer is sufficient to get me through most interviews, but it doesn't say anything about what I'd do in real life, let alone provide any clues about my attitude. There's a big difference between knowing the path and walking the path. (Do we really think smokers are somehow oblivious to the health effects of smoking? When I was younger, I knew darn well about the possible consequences, but that didn't stop me from putting Mr. Marlboro in my mouth.) The answer I gave reflects the fact that I know how to manage team conflict. But just because I know what to do doesn't preclude me from having a bad attitude, such as yelling at my team to get its act together because I can't control my temper. Or simply ignoring the problem and letting it fester and destroy the team because I'm too scared to deal with it, or whatever.

Over the years, I've met few leaders who didn't understand the idea that a toxic personality can destroy a work group. It's an intuitive and easily understood concept. And yet I've met thousands of managers who were afraid to sit down and have some straight talk with those same toxic personalities. The theory is simple and the hypotheticals are easy, but actually handling the situation can be terrifying. And that's the problem with hypotheticals—they're testing whether applicants understand the theory. They fail completely, though, when it comes to assessing whether candidates will actually implement that theory in the real world.

Leadership IQ conducted a study a few years ago called "Why CEOs Get Fired." My team and I went beyond the typical press release vagaries such as "Bob has decided to step down for personal reasons and we appreciate his years of service" and investigated the true reasons why CEOs get ousted. The study revealed that one of the top reasons CEOs get the boot is a lack of execution—too much talk and not enough action. They know what needs to be done; they just can't bring themselves to actually do it. Most executives are really smart, but that brainpower doesn't mean they always take the right actions (like avoiding petty power plays, or not becoming emotionally blind to failing pet projects or low performing executives).

So the next time you feel tempted to ask a job candidate "What would you do if two angry customers demanded your attention at the same time?" or "If selected for this position, how quickly could you make a significant contribution?" save yourself the time and trouble. Whatever answer you get is going to be a poor predictor of what that person would do in real life.

DON'T ASK THESE QUESTIONS NUMBER 4: THE UNDIFFERENTIATING QUESTIONS

As we've already established, an interview question is worth asking only if it differentiates between high and low performers. And, as I said earlier, if a question is designed so it allows every candidate to give roughly the same answer, it's analogous to giving a test on which everyone automatically gets the same grade. There's a corollary problem, though; essentially, it's as though you were giving a test without an answer key. If you ask an interview question and you have no clue how to use the answer as an indicator of high or low performance, what's the point of asking it? It's an undifferentiating question.

Here's an example. Imagine I ask everyone I interview to tell me their favorite flavor of pie. (Note that this question would probably never pass a review by your legal team, but it makes for a useful theoretical illustration.) Asking about pie is a ridiculous question, not just for the obvious and legal reasons, but also because I don't have any validating data. That is, I have no idea what it means if someone says "blueberry" or "banana cream." It could be a potentially valid question only if numerous scientific studies indicated that anyone whose favorite pie is strawberry-rhubarb is, say, an aspiring serial killer.

I say that only half-jokingly, because while the example is admittedly goofy, the research method is quite sound. For example, you may have heard of the "homicidal triad," which is three behaviors (animal cruelty, obsession with setting fires, and bed-wetting past age five) often thought to predict that someone is prone to homicidal behavior. This triad, also called the Macdonald Triad, was noticed by psychiatrist John M. Macdonald who discovered that sadistic psychiatric patients often had those three behaviors in common.

In essence, Dr. Macdonald did exactly what I'm talking about here with the favorite pie question. He looked at a population of people (violence-prone psychiatric patients for him, employees for me) and isolated common behaviors (torturing animals or loving blueberry pie). The problem is, unlike Dr. Macdonald, I have no evidence that links high performance with any particular kind of pie.

Now let's say I survey every employee in my organization and discover that all my high performers love cherry pie and hate apple pie. And then I discover that all my low performers love apple pie and hate cherry pie. Armed with this bit of insight, the question about pies might actually become useful (assuming my lawyers ever allowed me to ask it). But if I were able to ask it, then I could query candidates about their favorite pies, and if they said "cherry," I'd hire them on the spot. And if they said "apple," I'd end the interview immediately.

So what am I really saying here? Are questions like these good or bad? The answer is that these oddball questions are bad because there's no scientific evidence to correlate specific interview answers with real-life work behaviors. Too often interviewers get too cute. They think that because they're trying to figure out a person's attitude, they should design a clever, pseudo-psychological question that will reveal the person's personality. But they don't typically have any science to back this up. They just happen to like a particular question and so they stick with it, even if all it elicits is useless or incorrect information.

The following are a few examples of some particularly troublesome undifferentiating questions. These interview questions are actually being used. Some were sourced from the folks who have been certified in Hiring for Attitude or who have attended a Leadership IQ hiring webinar or seminar. I found others on Glassdoor.com. (Glassdoor.com is a free career community where anyone can find and anonymously share an inside look at jobs and companies.)

- "What do you like to do for fun?" (According to Glassdoor.com, this was an interview question for an intern at Ernst & Young. A related question is "What do you like to do outside of work?")
- "How are M&M's made?" (According to Glassdoor .com, this was an interview question asked by US Bank.)
- "If you could be any superhero, who would it be?" (According to Glassdoor.com, this was an interview question asked by AT&T, but we've also been told this question—or the variation "Which superpower would you choose?"—has been asked by companies like Citigroup.)
- "What was the last book you read?" (We've heard hundreds of reports of companies using this question, including Humana and Fujitsu Network Communications. The "movie" variation is also popular.)
- "Which one of the seven dwarves would you be?" (Honestly, it just seems too cruel to name the companies that use this question.)
- "If you could be any kind of tree (or animal/fish/vegetable), what kind of tree would you be?" (We've also heard of hundreds of companies using these questions.)

So let's suppose I ask my candidates the question "If you could be any kind of animal, what kind of animal would you be?" Once again, without any scientific studies to prove that every high performer in my company answers this question "lion," and every low performer answers "gazelle," I just don't gain a lot of insight. And even worse, the insight I think I'm getting could be completely wrong. What if I think all high performers would answer "parrot" (because I'm a huge Jimmy Buffett fan) and all low performers would answer "lizard" (no offense intended to any Jim Morrison fans)? How many wrong people will I hire simply because they too like parrots? And, how many stars might get cast aside because they happen to like reptiles?

I actually had an executive from a well-known energy company tell me that his hiring managers regularly use the animal question. The top executives decided, without any scientific study, that future high performers would say "tiger" and future low performers would say "elephant." And they stood by those answers—if you didn't say tiger, it wasn't likely that you were going to get hired. Just imagine how many potential high performers they passed over (and how many low performers they hired) because of an answer to an undifferentiating question.

And just for the record (not that it really matters as the question is null and void regardless), tigers may be cool (after all, Charlie Sheen has tiger blood in his veins), but elephants happen to be far smarter. In fact, the rundown of animal intelligence is often listed as humans, followed by apes, followed by elephants, followed by dolphins. And it's not just because of the elephant's famed ability to remember. Even Aristotle once said the elephant was ". . . the beast which passeth all others in wit and mind." So I can only assume the interviewers at that energy company did no research at all when they came up with the right and wrong answers to their senseless question. Because if you were going to pull some nonsensical "right answer" out of thin air, wouldn't you at least want the smarter, more loyal, longer-living, no-natural-predators animal?

Let me offer one more critical thought on these types of questions. Many of the pseudo-psychological questions such as "What's the last book you read?" open the door to potential legal problems. For example, pretend you work at a publicly traded nonreligious, but fairly conservative, organization, and you ask the last book question. Now let's say you have a technically qualified candidate who answers, "Gee, the last book I read was *Practicing Your Faith as a Litigious Bisexual Wiccan Cancer Patient.*" What do you do with that answer? In the worst-case scenario, you've potentially gleaned three bits of information—sexual preference, religion, and medical status—all of which are illegal to go after in an interview. And for what purpose did you put yourself in that kind of dangerous position? You didn't learn anything useful about this candidate, did you? And if the revealing part of that book title reflects the candidate's personality, you've got a potential legal problem should you decide not to hire this person.

Bad interview questions can be crazy, funny, and even illegal, but they all share a common link: they don't do anything to help you assess attitude. For that you need Brown Shorts questions, so let's get started learning how to create them.

For free downloadable resources including the latest research, discussion guides, and forms please visit www.leadershipiq.com/hiring.

3

How to Create Brown Shorts Interview Questions

Now that you know which interview questions not to ask, it's time to figure out which ones you should ask. Quite simply, you're going to ask Brown Shorts questions. The Brown Shorts Discovery you completed earlier allowed you to dig deep into your organizational culture. And you should now have a list of the critical high and low performer attitudes that predict success and failure in your organization. The Brown Shorts questions you're about to create will present candidates with situations selected specifically around those attitudes. Using these custom-built questions, you will surreptitiously pressure candidates to abandon their prepared answers and carefully rehearsed scripts. What you'll hear instead is the raw truth from people about how they have reacted to those attitude-based situations in the past. And once you measure their responses against the real-life performance of your best (and worst) people with the Answer Guidelines you'll create in the next chapter, you'll have a clear picture of what each candidate would be like when working for your company.

Brown Shorts Interview Questions reveal the truth about attitude so masterfully that it doesn't take many of them to get the job done. In fact, most interviewers who have been certified in Hiring for Attitude report that five or six questions are all they use. And the before and after numbers reflect the impact the Brown Shorts questions have had on those organizations' hiring success.

Let's take an example that you wouldn't normally hear about in a business book. MOKA is a nonprofit charitable agency and a regional leader in serving people with disabilities in western Michigan. It's not as famous an organization as Southwest or Microchip, but that doesn't make it any less worthy. MOKA provides individual job placement, residential and community living support, independent living training, and support for the families of children with autism and other disabilities. The agency was kind enough to share the following data about its experiences using Brown Shorts questions.

MOKA is somewhat unique in hiring research because it had two different hiring programs that opened within approximately six to eight months of each other, both in the same geographic location. Program A utilized MOKA's Brown Shorts questions, but Program B had not yet developed the questions. So it was an interesting test to compare the Brown Shorts method against a control group.

Program A (the Brown Shorts group) had a 33 percent turnover rate in the first six months after hiring. All of those people resigned. By contrast, Program B (without the Brown Shorts questions) had a 54 percent turnover. And of those 54 percentage points, 31 were resignations and the other 23 were discharges. That's a striking comparison. Turnover was far smaller with the Brown Shorts hiring method and there were no terminations.

MOKA's hiring process also tracks conditional job offers, the period occurring after the interview but before the candidate passes the background checks. The Brown Shorts group lost only one person in that stage, but the non-Brown Shorts group lost six people.

This was MOKA's first time using Brown Shorts questions and I'd say they did a heck of a job. And personally, while I love seeing our clients achieve record profits with Brown Shorts hiring, I'm also thrilled that Brown Shorts made a difference in the lives of families of children with disabilities.

CREATING YOUR BROWN SHORTS QUESTIONS: A FOUR-STEP PROCESS

Creating your Brown Shorts questions couldn't be easier. Just follow the four-step process shown in Figure 3.1 for each question you create.

Let's walk through the four steps one by one.

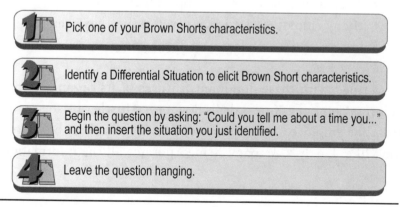

Figure 3.1. The Four-Step Brown Shorts Process

Brown Shorts Question Step 1: Pick One of Your Brown Shorts Characteristics

The first step is choosing one of the Brown Shorts characteristics you defined during your Brown Shorts Discovery. For example, observe Company X, which is driven by a highly Social Culture. Theirs is an open, creative community; ideas are freely shared, and feedback is generously swapped.

As part of its Brown Shorts Discovery, the company interviewed key executives and managers and identified the following behavioral markers about its culture:

- Departments are highly collaborative.
- Employees are respected as individuals.
- Employees show their unfinished work for feedback without fear of ridicule or demotion.
- Employees accept total responsibility for their work without excuses.
- Employees share what they've learned with their colleagues so all can acquire new skills.
- There are no nasty office politics.
- Interpersonal harmony is critically important.
- There's little sense of self-importance.
- If any employees are jerks—even if they have genius ideas—they won't last long at the company.

Armed with these dominant features of its organizational culture, Company X next drills down even further by surveying frontline employees to get the specifics of what these behaviors look like. Lastly, Company X incorporates all the information gathered into two lists: the positive Brown Shorts (attitudes that differentiate high performers) and the negative Brown Shorts (low performer attitudes that don't fit the culture). Table 3.1 summarizes what Company X found out.

All Company X needs to do to complete Step 1 of the Brown Shorts question process is to choose one of these Brown Shorts characteristics.

Table 3.1.   Company X's Brown Shorts

Positive Brown Shorts	Negative Brown Shorts
High performers are highly collaborative. They help each other out without being asked, and without any expectation of recognition or reward.	Low performers routinely want individual recognition rather than share recognition with the larger team.
High performers share constructive thoughts and reactions without making their colleagues defensive, angry, or embarrassed.	Low performers share constructive ideas in ways that belittle, embarrass, or anger their colleagues.
High performers take personal responsibility for the quality and timeliness of their work without blame or excuses. If they do have problems, they solve them and then they share the problems and solutions with others so that everyone else can learn from their issues.	Low performers blame others—colleagues and customers—when things go wrong, and say things like "I couldn't get it done because . . ." or "It's somebody else's fault."
High performers are self-directed learners. If they don't know how to do something, they actively find the necessary information or other resources to help them gain the skills and knowledge they need.	Low performers have a negative disposition. When faced with a new situation they regularly respond with the reasons why something will *not* work rather than try to figure out ways to achieve success.

Brown Shorts Question Step 2:
Identify a Differential Situation to Elicit
Brown Shorts Characteristics

When you compare and contrast the positive and negative Brown Shorts lists shown earlier, it's obvious that high performers and low performers at Company X respond very differently when faced with similar situations. When faced with an opportunity for recognition, the high performers demure while low performers step on anyone in order to get that notice or reward. When things go wrong, high performers aren't interested in finding a source of blame; they stay focused on finding a solution. Low performers, in contrast, are quick to blame others and eager to escape accountability. And when high performers in this unique culture are asked to do something they don't know how to do, they actively acquire new skills. Low performers, on the other hand, immediately throw up their hands, resist, and complain.

We call these "Differential Situations" because they're the moments when the differences between high and low performers are most starkly in contrast. And this contrast is what you want, because situations in which high and low performers respond similarly are of no use in determining attitude. It may be that both your high and low performers like maple trees, or read John Grisham novels, or say that they "care too much" when asked about their biggest weakness. High and low performers may answer lots of traditional interview questions the same way. Brainteaser questions—why are manhole covers round or how many gas stations are in Los Angeles—are notoriously bad at differentiating high and low performers because many smart people ace brainteasers but still have terrible attitudes. These aren't the kinds of situations we're looking for here. We want only Differential Situations.

The ultimate test of a great interview question is the extent to which it differentiates between high and low performers. So if the situation you're asking about doesn't elicit different responses from high and low performers, ditch that question— it's a waste of your time. When Leadership IQ consults with organizations to design their interview questions, we sometimes find that some executive is fixated on sticking with his or her pet question. In these cases, we conducted a study of the organization's interviews to see whether that question is actually generating differentiated responses from high and low performers. Most people won't take medicine that hasn't been scientifically shown to be beneficial. However, when it comes to interview questions, most companies are asking away without any validation whatsoever.

Getting back to Company X, our Brown Shorts Discovery tells us that high and low performers respond differently when facing problems, receiving credit, responding to significant changes in the workplace, working cross-functionally, and learning new skills. High and low performers also respond differently when they encounter failure; for example, how they respond to a situation where they try to fix or improve something and they just can't get their solution to work.

How can I be so sure that high and low performers will exhibit different behaviors in these situations? First, during the Brown Shorts Discovery I would have observed the behaviors directly, from the interviews, and from survey responses. Second, during the course of those interviews and surveys I ask,

"What are some situations in which these attitudes manifest themselves?" You can see how this works by using the Brown Shorts characteristics Company X lists to reflect the attitudes of high and low performers when those employees don't know how to do something.

> **High performers:** They're self-directed learners, and if they don't know how to do something, they actively find the information or other resources they need.
>
> **Low performers:** They have a negative disposition, and when faced with a new situation, they regularly respond with reasons why something will *not* work rather than try to figure out ways to achieve success.

Given these descriptions, what are some likely scenarios where these high performers will really show off their great attitudes? That is, in what situations will they roll up their sleeves and actively find information? I imagine we'd see these qualities when they're given an assignment they don't know how to do, when they're asked to do something outside their job description, when they have to unexpectedly fill in for somebody else, or when they encounter a customer problem they've never seen before.

And when will low performers really show off their bad attitudes? Well, probably in any of the situations I just mentioned. Any time low performers are asked to change a procedure, learn a new technology, or solve a problem that really isn't within their official responsibilities, they will dig in their heels and explain why it can't be done. As I noted a few paragraphs ago, you will see both high and low performer attitudes on display when these folks face failure, such as when they try to fix or improve something and they just can't get their solution to work.

Now that we've got some Differential Situations to work with, we need to choose one of them and build a Brown Shorts question around it. I'm personally partial to the situation where people have faced failure, but when you create these questions in your organization, you should pick the situations that your employees face most frequently.

Brown Shorts Question Step 3: Begin the Question by Asking "Could You Tell Me About a Time You . . ." and Then Insert the Differential Situation You Just Identified

The third step in creating your Brown Shorts question is to begin with the phrase "Could you tell me about a time you . . ." and then finish the question by inserting the Differential Situation you just identified. So Company X's Brown Shorts question would be something like "Could you tell me about a time you tried to fix or improve something but your solution just didn't work?" I told you this was going to be easy.

Brown Shorts Question Step 4: Leave the Question Hanging

Finally, in the fourth step, you must leave your Brown Shorts question hanging. In Chapter 2 I pointed out some problems with many behavioral interview questions and noted that one of the worst things you can do is to finish off a question with a leading phrase such as ". . . and how did you overcome that?"

or ". . . and how did you solve that challenge?" There's a natural tendency to want to grammatically resolve these questions, and you're going to have to fight that. For instance, when I hear "Could you tell me about a time you faced competing priorities . . ." I instinctively want to add ". . . and how you balanced them?" But I know that adding such a phrase will make this a leading question and destroy its effectiveness, so I resist the urge.

Could You . . .

The words we choose to begin the question with are another important issue. Many commonly used behavioral interview questions begin with the phrase "Tell me about a time. . . ." But Brown Shorts questions preface that with "Could you tell me . . ." in order to control the question and let the candidate feel like he or she has some measure of control in the interview process.

People are generally pretty guarded when they're in an interview. They may seem perfectly open, jovial, and relaxed, but that just means they're good performers. When I'm speaking to an audience of 1,000 people, I may appear relaxed and fun loving. But in reality, my mind is hard at work, carefully choosing each word that comes out of my mouth. My main focus is on making sure that what I'm saying has maximum impact on my audience. People interviewing for a job (especially the smart ones) are just as focused on what they say, so you want to get them to loosen up and lower their guard. Give them the feeling that they have more control in this process so it feels less like an exam and more like a conversation, and you'll be surprised at the information you'll uncover.

When people are being hammered with questions, especially questions that start to sound like orders—"Tell me about situation A, then you will tell me about situation B"—it constantly reminds them that they are in a powerless position, and that everything they say is being critically judged. As a result, they become guarded and reticent in what they are willing to share. In order to get people to open up in their responses, you want them to forget that they're in a position without much power. Instead, you want them to feel that this is more like a conversation with a new friend.

So "Could you tell me . . .?" is a subtle way of saying "You have control because you can choose whether or not you want to answer this question." Of course, no one is actually going to refuse to answer the question (unless they really don't want the job). But just suggesting they have a choice in the matter plants a psychological seed that they have more control, as if they were conversing with a friend. They start to act more like they would in a friendly conversation (open and honest). Plus, remember that "Tell me about . . ." is not exactly a question; it's an order that requires a response, and that's always going to put people on guard.

Every good clinical psychologist who deals with young kids knows that you can force your kids to get in the car by saying "Get in the car now!" But it's a lot easier, and faster, to instead say "You can get in the car by yourself, or I can help you get in the car. It's your choice." Kids love this because it really does feel like a choice to them. You know it's not really a choice, just as you know answering the interview question isn't really a choice, but it feels like a choice to the person on the other end of those words. And when we're talking about interpersonal communication, perception truly is reality.

Finally, the specific words you select and how you choose to say them does matter in hiring. You can't just read from a bad script and expect that you're going to make great hires.

This is a battle where subtlety matters, small words make a big difference, and your performance is critical. That's why Leadership IQ has a certification program to become a Certified Interviewer. It takes more than 15 minutes to do this really well.

So to recap, the four-step process for creating your own Brown Shorts Interview Questions is:

Step 1: Pick one of your Brown Shorts characteristics.
High performers are self-directed learners, and if they don't know how to do something, they actively find the necessary information or other resources to help them.

Step 2: Identify a Differential Situation to elicit Brown Shorts characteristics. When they need to fix or improve something, do they try to solve the problem or simply complain that it can't be done.

Step 3: Begin the question by asking "Could you tell me about a time you. . . ." and then insert the situation you just identified. "Could you tell me about a time you tried to fix or improve something, but it just didn't work?"

Step 4: Leave the question hanging. "Could you tell me about a time you tried to fix or improve something, but it just didn't work?" Resist the urge to add "and what did you do?"

We know from Company X's Brown Shorts Discovery that when they ask a Brown Shorts question, they are going to hear a noticeable difference in how prospective high performers and likely low performers respond. (And their customized answer key makes recognizing that difference an easy task.)

When one of Leadership IQ's clients recently asked the interview question "Could you tell me about a time you tried to fix or improve something, but it just didn't work?" These are some of the actual responses they got from likely low performers:

> I was trying to fix a problem with our XXX product. I was going to fix it my way, but then my boss had some supposedly brilliant idea for fixing it. Of course, it failed just like I knew it would. So I tried to get my boss to let me fix it my way, but, big surprise, he said no. It was a great idea, though, and it would have worked. I mean, what can you do when your boss just has no interest in good ideas? Although it probably doesn't really matter, because even if he had used my idea, God knows I wouldn't have gotten credit for it anyway.

> My rule is that even when something isn't working, you just never admit you don't know the answer. Placate, adjust the truth, lie—whatever it takes to keep the situation under wraps. Or even better, just stay quiet until you can find the right answer, which will hopefully fall into your lap at some point.

> At my last job I was flooded with requests to fix pretty intractable problems. I am always fairly cautious when it comes to stepping outside my comfort zone, so I just turned these situations over to the support department. That's what they're there for—to solve problems that nobody else wants to.

Wow. Every time I read those responses, or ones like them, I'm grateful I don't have to work with those people. In contrast, answers from the probable high performers sounded very different. Here are a few snippets from their responses.

Once I tried to fix an issue at my other job. However, the fix turned out not to be such a good idea. Even though it didn't work, it was a good experience to go through and I was able to learn from it. I asked other employees if they had suggestions for improvement, and then I went back to the drawing table to come up with another solution. I've learned to investigate more thoroughly before taking steps to change a process and to involve my colleagues when I can because they've really got some great ideas. There's always somebody who has seen a similar situation who can readily point out the potential landmines.

We were having significant problems with a new software design, and every fix I tried failed. So I involved many more folks on our team and I asked a lot of questions. I made sure to spread out my questions over many resources so I didn't burden any one individual.

I was given the task of assembling some very specific quality data for a report, but none of the queries I ran generated the necessary data. I recruited the help of someone in QA who knew the data, the technology, and the right format. I didn't waste company resources trying to recreate this thing from the ground up and was able to leverage someone else's knowledge. Plus it was nice to share the credit for doing a great job.

Once again, wow. I now have a clear idea of whom, among all these candidates, I do and do not want on my team.

WHAT ABOUT PROBLEM SOLVERS AND PROBLEM BRINGERS?

Remember earlier in the chapter when I distinguished between problem bringers and problem solvers? One thing you probably noticed about the sample responses to this Brown Shorts question is that the wrong attitude answers generally described a problem but never referenced how the issue was ultimately solved. It either remained unresolved or became somebody else's problem. In contrast, the right attitude answers talked about an initial failure but then went on to describe how the person overcame the failure to eventually solve the problem.

When you ask a question like "Could you tell me about a time you tried to fix or improve something, but it just didn't work?" some people assume that you want to hear about a situation that was never fixed. But that's not what the question actually asked. What you really asked was for the candidate to describe a time he tried to fix something, but it just didn't work. That could easily be interpreted to mean that a solution he tried didn't work, which leaves open the possibility that he tried a different solution that did work. It all depends on how you look at this question, and I wrote the question specifically to allow for multiple interpretations.

Problem-solver personalities simply can't bring themselves to think about a situation as a total failure. They need to keep trying and eventually solve it or at least salvage some useful lesson. And you will generally hear that underlying interpretation in the responses problem solvers provide, just as you'll hear the opposite in the answers from the problem bringers.

Your Brown Shorts Discovery has already uncovered all the information you need to create your Brown Shorts Interview Questions. The more you repeat the process by creating a Brown Shorts question for each of the attitudes that reflect your positive and negative Brown Shorts, the easier it will become.

Just remember the four steps and you'll get it right every time.

Step 1: Pick one of your Brown Shorts characteristics.

Step 2: Identify a Differential Situation to elicit Brown Shorts characteristics.

Step 3: Begin the question by asking, "Could you tell me about a time you . . ." and then insert the situation you just identified.

Step 4: Leave the question hanging.

More Examples of Brown Shorts Interview Questions

Step 1: If you go back to the Brown Shorts Discovery findings for Company X, you'll find that high performers take personal responsibility for the quality and timeliness of their work without blame or excuses. By contrast, low performers usually blame others, including customers.

Step 2: A Differential Situation that's likely to distinguish between high and low performers in Company X is the challenge faced when dealing with a difficult customer.

Step 3: Ask the question "Could you tell me about a customer you found particularly difficult to work with?"

Step 4: Always make sure that nothing in your Brown Shorts question will lead the candidate to give the "right" answer.

Here again are some actual snippets of "wrong attitude" answers to the Brown Shorts question "Could you tell me about a customer you found particularly difficult to work with?"

- "Some customers act like you really have nothing better to do than spend all day solving their issues. There's no way to have a good relationship with someone like that."
- "This one client basically knew nothing about his industry and kept blaming our products for his failures. I finally had to tell him that he was not as smart as he thought he was. Big egos are always a challenge to work with."

And here are some snippets from actual "right attitude" answers.

- "A customer called and as soon as I answered the phone, he let loose a string of obscenities. Hidden among the cursing was the very real situation that they were going to miss an important meeting because of a problem with one of our products. It wasn't hard for me to see that the pressure was breaking him and he wasn't anywhere close to his normal self. So I didn't take any of the anger personally. We hopped on a web conference together and worked into the night to solve the issue. Out of gratitude (and perhaps a bit of embarrassment at snapping so ferociously) he's now one of my best customers."
- "I made a mistake and gave a customer the wrong reports. They fired us as their vendor on the spot, seemingly giving us no chance to make things right. I went to their office the next day, met with the

CEO and the team, and said "I'm sorry." I didn't offer any excuses or blame anybody else, I took full accountability for the mistake. They were surprised, and appreciative, and we saved the business relationship. We're their vendor again, and they're a very good customer."

The difficult customer question is a great one to ask, but you're not going to know the value of the answers you get in response to it unless you know your Brown Shorts. What constitutes resolving difficult customer issues in one company might be a total failure in another company. Southwest Airlines and The Ritz-Carlton, for example, are both great companies, but their approaches to solving customer issues are different, as are their cultures and business models.

Here's another example:

Step 1: Imagine your Brown Shorts Discovery identified that high performers consistently maintain a positive and cheerful affect even in the face of failure and other difficult situations. In contrast, low performers maintain a negative disposition, and when faced with tough situations, they find reasons why something will *not* work rather than try to figure out ways to make it succeed.

Step 2: There are many potential Differential Situations that could be used to assess this characteristic. If I think about episodes when negative people loudly displayed their negativity, I might list someone getting an assignment she didn't think would succeed, or that she didn't agree with. Perhaps she was asked to participate in a change effort, was given a tough deadline, worked on a team with someone she didn't particularly like, or she faced competing priorities.

Step 3: Any of these Differential Situations could work well for a Brown Shorts question. So depending on the exact situations your people face on the job, you could ask questions such as:

- Could you tell me about a time when your boss gave you an assignment that didn't seem to make much sense?
- Could you tell me about a time when you were given an assignment that you were sure wasn't going to succeed?
- Could you tell me about a time when you were struggling to meet a commitment you had made to a customer or colleague?

I'll show you some actual answers to questions like these in an upcoming chapter. But like the other examples I've shared, they really do differentiate between people with the right and wrong attitudes.

Here are a few more examples of some Brown Shorts Interview Questions.

Example 1: If your Brown Shorts Discovery reveals that high performers never say "That's not my job," but low performers utter that phrase regularly, you could ask "Could you tell me about a time when you were given an assignment that really didn't fall within your role?" This is a Differential Situation that everyone who's ever held a job has faced.

Example 2: If your Brown Shorts Discovery reveals
that high performers are highly adept at overcoming
impediments to working across functional and
geographic boundaries, whereas low performers hit a
roadblock and give up, you could ask "Could you tell
me about a time when working across departmental,
divisional, or regional lines was challenging?"

Example 3: If your Brown Shorts Discovery reveals that
high performers generate ideas that are unique and
out of the box, while low performers recycle the same
thoughts as everyone else, you could ask "Could you
tell me about a time when you had to think outside the
box?"

HOW TALL IS TALL?

The questions I listed previously raise an important issue that
I'll illustrate with an odd question directed at you. (This is
unrelated to interview questions, so bear with me.) I have a
very tall friend. How tall do *you* think he is? Over six feet
tall? Maybe 6'4"? 6'5"? Shorter? Taller? I know you don't have
enough information to accurately answer the question, but take
a guess anyway.

I've asked this question to thousands of people, and I've
consistently found that the answer depends largely on the height
of the person doing the answering. If a man is 5'7", he might
think that 6'0" is tall. My sister-in-law is 4'11" and she thinks
my 5'2" wife is tall. I'm 5'10" and have a friend whom I consider

as very tall at 6'4". However, he thinks "very tall" doesn't start until you hit 6'7". It's all in the perception of the beholder.

So why do I mention this? You probably noticed that some of the sample Brown Shorts questions are open to interpretation. Take, for example, the question "Could you tell me about a time when you had to think outside the box?" I could have an idea that I think is outside the box but that others at a high-tech start-up would consider stodgy and inside the box. However, that very same idea could be too far outside the box at a more conservative organization. It's all in the eye of the beholder— and dependent upon your unique corporate culture.

Asking Brown Shorts questions that are open to interpretation provides a clear view of the candidate's standards. I could ask somebody an open question such as "Could you tell me about your proudest accomplishment this year?" If the response is "I showed up for work on time more than half of the days," well, I just learned that this person has very low standards when it comes to feeling pride. But if somebody else answered with "Even though I received 28 patents and doubled the size of the company, I'm not ready to feel proud because I really should have done more," I just learned that this person has really high standards when it comes to feeling pride.

This same lesson applies to every question I've shared. When I ask "Could you tell me about a customer you found particularly difficult to work with?" it silently begs the question "what do you consider difficult?" When I ask "Could you tell me about a time when you were struggling to meet a commitment you had made to a customer or colleague?" the candidate's response will tell me what he considers "struggling" or what she thinks a "tough deadline" is.

The bottom line is that you really need your Brown Shorts Answer Guidelines to correctly interpret the responses you get to your Brown Shorts Interview Questions. We will be covering all that in Chapter 4. But first we need to review the Coachability Question.

THE COACHABILITY QUESTION

A large part of this book has been devoted to showing you how to create specific Brown Shorts Interview Questions for your unique organizational culture. But there is one universal interview question that can be used in almost every organization and culture.

Think back to the beginning of the book. I noted that a Leadership IQ study on hiring failures discovered that the single biggest reason that new hires fail is a lack of coachability. In all the work Leadership IQ has done in designing Brown Shorts interview processes for our clients, we've never seen an organization where coachability wasn't a pertinent and valuable characteristic. The following paragraphs describe a question that every organization can use to assess coachability—what I somewhat unimaginatively call the Coachability Question.

The Coachability Question has five parts, and each part must be asked in order and exactly as I describe it here. Yes, it's a robust question. But when you combine it with your Brown Shorts questions, you will learn more about candidates' attitudes than you would ever have thought possible.

The five parts of the Coachability Question are as follows:

1. What was your boss's name? Please spell the full name for me.
2. Tell me about _____ *(name)* _____ as a boss.
3. What's something that you could have done (or done differently) to enhance your working relationship with _____ *(name)* _____ ?
4. When I talk to _____ *(name)* _____ , what will he or she tell me your strengths are?
5. Now all people have areas where they can improve, so when I talk to _____ *(name)* _____ , what will he or she tell me your weaknesses are?

Knowing these five parts doesn't really help you understand the logic behind the Coachability Question. So let's walk through each part for a better idea of how the whole thing works.

Coachability Question Step 1: Make Them Believe You're Going to Talk with Their Previous Boss

The Coachability Question begins by asking the candidate for the full name of his present or most recent boss "What was your boss's name?" Sometimes when a candidate is currently employed, he doesn't want to share that name; in those cases, just go with the name of the boss from the previous job.

Once you've got the name (Kate Johnson), get the spelling of the name: "Please spell the full name for me."

In doing this, you lead the candidate to believe you're actually going to call Kate. The logic here is that nobody would waste time confirming the spelling of a name in such a detailed manner if she weren't actually planning to contact that person (at least that's what you want the candidate to think). And having the candidate believe you're actually going to call a boss for a reference is great motivation to give truthful responses.

I want to reinforce the point about the spelling because interviewers are most likely to skip this seemingly simple step. The common misconception is that because it's a small step, it's inconsequential, and because it's outside what most interviewers do, it's somewhat uncomfortable. But the Coachability Question will not work if you don't confirm the spelling of the name. This little psychological twist makes this whole process so revealing.

It's also important to use the language I've given here: "Please spell the full name for me." Note that this is not exactly a question, but rather a stated request. It's fairly formal language (more formal than "how do you spell that?") and signals a seriousness on your part about contacting that boss.

Coachability Question Step 2: Ask Them to Describe Their Boss

Simply ask "So tell me about what Kate was like as a boss." The response will give you some hints about what this person is looking for in a boss. If the answer is "Kate was a very hands-on manager and wanted regular updates," and the words are delivered in a clipped manner and with a hint of a frown, you can pretty safely infer that this candidate doesn't like that style of management. If someone indicates (either implicitly or explicitly) that he doesn't respond well to micromanagers, and you're a bit of a micromanager, you need to ask yourself whether you could successfully manage this person. But if someone's last boss sounds like you, and it appears that she loved working for that person, then that's a good sign.

Now, regardless of whether the response is positive or negative, many people have received training that teaches them never to talk about their last boss. This means you often won't get a complete response on the first try. And that's why you might need the following two probing questions about their former boss.

- What's something you wish Kate had done more of?
- What's something you wish Kate had done less of?

These two questions are simple but powerful. Even when a person has been coached not to speak about the boss, these two questions manage to skate under the typical interviewee's defenses. They're not talking about the actual boss but instead about what the employee could have used more and less of from that boss in order to have been more effective.

So ask these two probes, one after the other, and you'll hear specific information about what this person needs from a manager in order to be a successful employee. That answer is an absolute gold mine of information about whether you'll actually be able to manage that person effectively.

Coachability Question Step 3: Ask What They Personally Could Have Done Differently

So far we've been asking the candidate about a former boss, and that's an important relationship to know about. But as the Coachability Question ultimately gauges the candidate's coachability, we also want to assess to what extent the candidate feels personally accountable for his or her own success. And this entails asking "What's something that you could have done (or done differently) to enhance your working relationship with _____Kate_____?"

High performers have high levels of critical self-awareness, which includes the ability to look critically at their own performance and see as many, if not more, flaws than anyone else. This is part of the very definition of coachability. If someone can't fathom what could have been done differently to make things better (even if things were already fantastic), then you know this person has no upside for additional improvement. It's a natural law of the universe that everyone has the potential for more improvement, no matter how good a person already is. The real question is whether someone is personally aware that this room for improvement exists.

Another thing you want to learn is whether or not the candidate takes any ownership for creating and maintaining a healthy relationship with the boss. The best candidates will not only tell you about the ownership they've taken but will also tell you about what personal changes they made since working with that boss. High performers don't just talk about what they could do to improve; they actually go and do it.

Coachability Question Step 4: Ask Them What Their Boss Considered Their Strengths

This is easily done by asking "When I talk to Kate, what will she tell me are your biggest strengths?" This question has two purposes. First, before you start asking about someone's weaknesses, it's nice to start with a more pleasant question. Talking about strengths makes people feel less guarded, and it will help keep your candidates feeling comfortable and open in their communications with you.

Second, it gives you an honest look at the qualities your candidates like best about themselves. For instance, if someone talks about being process-oriented and very detailed in his work, and you're looking for an out of the box, big-picture thinker, you just learned something very valuable. Sometimes people ask whether this is the same as asking candidates to describe their strengths (one of the questions I suggest you never ask). The answer is no. If you ask people to describe their strengths, you're going to get a canned answer that reflects what the person thinks you want to hear, not what that person actually believes. But when you ask it this way, under the veil of honesty brought about by the belief that you're going to verify this with the last boss, you will hear a very different answer.

Coachability Question Step 5: Ask Them What Their Boss Considered Their Weaknesses

Again, this can be accomplished with a simple question such as "Now everyone has some weaknesses, so when I talk to Kate, what will she tell me yours are?" This is perhaps the most critical part of the five-step process, but it only works if you've completed the previous four steps. In fact, if you do the first four steps successfully (especially confirming the spelling of the boss's name in Step 1), you might be shocked at the level of honesty this last question elicits.

You want to listen to the response you get to this question on two levels. First, you're going to assess whether the weakness is something you can live with. For instance, if someone says she was criticized for lying, being too political, or not completing assignments on time, then you may have revealed that this person shares some negative Brown Shorts characteristics with your low performers. Remember, the focus of the Coachability Question is to determine if someone is coachable or not.

Second, if the response you get is "I can't think of any weaknesses," or something like "I honestly don't know what Kate thought about me," then you've hit upon the biggest warning sign that someone is not coachable. If that person didn't (or couldn't) hear the constructive feedback offered by a previous boss, what are the chances that you'll be successful giving that person feedback? People who can't hear and assimilate constructive criticism are not coachable. And even without formal conversations with the boss, if they can't put themselves in their boss's shoes and anticipate their assessment, they're not coachable.

It's a common misconception that coachability is only about the ability to hear and assimilate feedback. Coachability also involves the ability to anticipate feedback. Great performers (employees, musicians, and athletes) know when they've made a mistake. If Yo-Yo Ma misses a note, or Peyton Manning throws an interception, they know about it long before the conductor or coach does, and they can tell you exactly why that mistake happened. They can also tell you exactly what the conductor, coach, or boss will say. They know what that feedback will be before they even get it, and that's why elite performers often don't need to hear all the feedback about what went wrong—

they know it already—they just need corrective mentoring and suggestions for improvement. So if someone cannot anticipate what the boss would have said, it's a clear sign that person doesn't have the attitude of coachability you're looking for.

For free downloadable resources including the latest research, discussion guides, and forms please visit www.leadershipiq.com/hiring.

4

Creating Brown Shorts Answer Guidelines

Knowing how to ask insightful interview questions is a great skill. But knowing how to accurately evaluate the responses to those questions is an even better skill. Here's what I mean. Consider the question "Can black hole evaporation be reconciled with quantum mechanics?" I know it's a bit out there, but I've been told (by people who know) that it's a great physics question. I would appear highly intelligent if I were to ask it of a bunch of physicists at a cocktail party. Unfortunately, I don't know the answer (I'm not sure physicists do either), which limits my ability to evaluate and assess any responses. I'm not able to differentiate between a great answer, a plausible answer, and a terrible answer. And I might even get sucked into believing a completely implausible answer just because it's delivered in an eloquent and confident manner. (Much like the impressive and convincing demeanor the majority of job candidates assume during an interview.)

I'm not saying that knowing the answer in advance is a prerequisite for every query you make. There are plenty of times when it's perfectly OK to ask a question if you're unsure, or even clueless, as to the answer. However, interviewing job candidates is when you definitely want guidelines on what good and bad answers sound like before you ask the question. This is a tool that you want to put in the hands of every member of your hiring team.

The concept of using Answer Guidelines as part of the hiring process is revolutionary in the world of hiring. In fact, Leadership IQ is the only group I know of that teaches this technique. You can find a lot of people who want to teach you how to create interview questions (albeit incorrectly). But there's nobody else out there teaching how to create an answer key to those questions so you can accurately and consistently score the responses you get.

Let me share with you a recent experience with a Leadership IQ client that reinforces the need for Answer Guidelines. To give you some context, this was a large chemical company with lots of employees, many of them engineers. (I am being deliberately vague because I don't want them identified.) Leadership IQ had been engaged to conduct a Brown Shorts project for this client. At the point when this story takes place, we'd completed the Discovery process and identified their Brown Shorts. We wrote a set of Brown Shorts Interview Questions and created custom Answer Guidelines to score the candidate responses to those questions. All these materials had been reviewed and approved by the organization's executive team. So we were just entering the final phase of the project, the point where we go in and train all their hiring managers on how to implement these tools. (It's all well and good to have great tools. However, if you don't know how to use them . . .)

But before we started the formal training, I conducted a little experiment. As you'll see, it's an easy exercise. I encourage you to try it out with your own hiring team. First, I shared with the group the Brown Shorts Interview Question that had been developed during Discovery. "Could you tell me about a time when you didn't know how to do something that a customer was asking you to do?"

Everybody loved the question. But despite the group's enthusiasm for it, I felt certain that there were a number of different ideas floating around regarding what a good answer would sound like. I continued the exercise by asking the group to silently read an actual answer that had been documented during a recent interview. I didn't want any second party vocal inflection or phrasing to influence individual thinking. And I asked all the managers to refrain from any discussion after they were done reading it.

Then, based on what they had just read, I asked this group to rate the candidate with a view toward how well that person fit their organizational culture. They were instructed to use a numerical seven-point rating scale, where only the endpoints were labeled with 1 for "Poor Fit" and 7 for "Great Fit." (See Figure 4.1.) There were no rating definitions given for points 2 through 6. I'll explain why the rating scale was designed this way in Chapter 5.

Just to review, here's the Brown Shorts question again: "Could you tell me about a time when you didn't know how

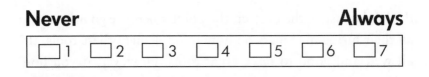

Figure 4.1.   The Seven-Point Scale

to do something that a customer was asking you to do?" And here's the answer that the candidate gave:

> At my last job I was inundated with requests that were outside my area of expertise or influence. I am always pretty cautious when it comes to stepping outside my comfort zone, so most of the time I just turned the situation over to someone more experienced. After all, I want to make sure I'm protecting the company's back because I don't want to touch a project for which I'm unqualified and then have it do damage to the client. The client's interests are always of paramount importance. And it's critical that an engineer adhere to accepted practices and the proper processes. If I'm in a situation where I don't know those processes, it's better for me to pass the request to someone else that does.

The managers participating in this exercise struggled to rate this candidate. The final numbers showed something really interesting; the scores ranged from 1 to 7, with everything in between. In a room of 50 managers, every number on that seven-point scale was chosen by at least two people. And remember, these managers were all employed by the same company, they all shared similar professional backgrounds, and they all worked for the same group of executives. But despite all these similarities, their assessment of the candidate showed that my initial suspicion had been right—every person in that room had a wildly different idea about what a good (or bad) answer sounded like. And did they ever become animated when I shared that fact with them!

I overheard one discussion between two guys sitting at the same table. I was told that their offices are located next door to each other and that they'd been good friends for years. Their conversation went something like this:

Manager A: "What's the matter with you? How could you score that answer a 6? This candidate would be a total failure here. He's all wrong for us!"

Manager B: "Sure, that's what you say. Because why would we want an engineer who actually followed a protocol!"

I asked the folks who gave the candidate a high score to tell me some of the things they liked about the answer:

- "This person is really focused on the customer. And you can tell extra care is being taken not to do anything that might damage our reputation with the customer."
- "This is someone who appreciates the proper engineering mind-set."
- "This sounds like someone who wants to protect the company."
- "I would much rather see someone be cautious than reckless in this kind of situation."

Then I asked the folks who skewered the candidate what they didn't like:

- "We're a company that always has to find solutions, no matter what; and this person just gives up the second something becomes what he or she considers too hard."
- "I don't like the 'inundated with requests' part. It makes me think that just about every request this person gets is going to be outside his or her comfort zone."
- "I was really turned off by the admission of 'I just turned the situation over to someone else.' Also, there was zero mention of keeping the customer in the loop."
- "I can handle the bringing in somebody else with more expertise part, but what bothers me is that I see no initiative to learn those new skills so that next time this person does know what to do and doesn't have to rely on outside help."

The results of this exercise highlight two big problems that organizations face when they Hire For Attitude without using Answer Guidelines. First off, you can usually find something you like, and something you dislike, in virtually every person you interview. (Of course, given that the consequences of hiring a bad attitude are worse than not hiring a good attitude, I'm more concerned about the former.) So without having some foundation to orient us and to tell us what good and bad answers sound like, it's awfully hard to evaluate candidates consistently and correctly.

The second big problem is the extent to which everybody involved in your hiring process does (or does not) understand your Brown Shorts. It may seem absurd, but there are a lot of people in your organization, including leaders, who don't know, or can't articulate, what makes your culture special. Similarly, they can't clearly tell you what separates your high and low performers.

This problem is not exclusively related to Brown Shorts. We conducted a study on whether employees understand their company's strategy. Using data from Leadership IQ's employee engagement survey, we assessed more than 70,000 employees on the extent to which they felt they could clearly articulate their organization's goals for the year. Only 34 percent felt they could clearly articulate those goals. And it gets worse because next we took part of that 34 percent and asked them to go ahead and actually articulate the goals. According to the supervisors who graded their answers, only about half of them really knew the goals. This left us with only 17 percent of employees who could correctly articulate their organization's goals. And while it's possible that some people actually could articulate the goals but rated themselves low because they didn't feel confident, my experience tells me that's not a large percentage of employees.

How are you supposed to achieve a strategy when nobody on your team knows what that strategy is? It reminds me of the old joke: the bad news is we're lost, but the good news is that we're making great time.

Strategies, Brown Shorts, Mission Statements—they're all susceptible to wrong interpretation. I recently gave a speech at a hospital's leadership retreat about how to translate your strategy into the front lines. After I finished, the CEO was so pumped up by what I'd said that he pulled $1,000 cash out of his pocket and offered it to the first manager who could correctly write down the company Mission Statement. Guess how many were able to do it?

Out of the 150 leaders in the room, not one answered correctly. Nobody got the $1,000, and the really sad part is that the company's Mission Statement is only 12 words long. As a reference, the Pledge of Allegiance contains 31 words. The real kicker, though, is that their Mission Statement is printed on the back of the name badge worn by every employee. But these folks were at an off-site retreat so they weren't wearing their badges.

Too often we take our Brown Shorts for granted. "Well of course we know who we are," we say, along with "and I can tell you exactly what differentiates our high and low performers." But it's always useful to see to what extent everybody agrees about that. If you went around the table at your next executive team meeting and asked each person to list the top three characteristics that differentiate high and low performers at your company, would each person have the same answer? What if you conducted this exercise at your next manager meeting? Or at an employee town hall?

The hiring managers at the chemical company where I conducted this exercise certainly didn't use the same high and low performer characteristics to rate their candidate. But that inconsistency wasn't because they weren't living and breathing their Brown Shorts every single day. Rather, it was because they hadn't yet learned to distill their Brown Shorts so they could explicitly say "These are the five characteristics that predict success or failure and that will let us measure every candidate accordingly."

Two of the numerous Brown Shorts we identified during that chemical company's Discovery stood out (and are especially appropriate for driving this all home).

- You take ownership of problems—even if you're not the one who will ultimately fix it, you shepherd the process until it's resolved.
- You're a self-directed learner—you take full responsibility for growing and developing your skills, and while you may not learn everything, you're in a constant state of growth.

Even if you lack any other knowledge about the organization, you now know that these two characteristics drive the success of its best people. You can easily assess the answer to a question such as "Tell me about a time when you didn't know how to do something that a boss or customer was asking you to do." And you can easily recognize that the sample answer I passed around that day clearly revealed that the candidate in question was a poor cultural fit. There just wasn't much ownership, self-directed learning, or desire for personal growth in that answer.

Hiring for Attitude requires both your Brown Shorts and your Brown Shorts Interview Questions. But in order to make it all work, you also need your Brown Shorts Answer Guidelines. That way, when you (and every member of your hiring team) are in the middle of a live interview, you'll know exactly what you should be listening for and how you should react when you hear it.

Let's get started creating your Answer Guidelines.

BROWN SHORTS ANSWER GUIDELINES

So exactly what are Brown Shorts Answer Guidelines? They are really quite simple and contained in one document. That written document considers, one-by-one, each of your Brown Shorts Interview Questions. After each question comes a list of good answers (called Positive Signals) and a list of bad answers (called Warning Signs). There's also a scoring form, which we'll address in Chapter 5.

Before we dive into how to formulate your questions, here's an abbreviated version of one organization's Brown Shorts Answer Guidelines. This will allow you to become familiar with the basic format you're going to use in creating your own answer guidelines.

Brown Shorts Interview Question
Tell me about a time when you didn't know how to do
    something that a boss or customer was asking you to do.

Warning signs: These types of answers can indicate a poor fit with the organization's culture.

- "When I don't know how to do something I just placate the requestor and obfuscate the issue until hopefully it starts to go away. I've found it to be pretty common for a customer or boss who gets all hot and bothered over an issue to completely forget it within 72 hours."
- "I had one boss who was terrible at communication, and a lot of times it negatively affected the procedures

and work flow in our department. I know it really impacted my work and made my life pretty miserable. There were a lot of times when I didn't find out about process changes until after the fact. This slowed me up a lot, and I spent many days just frozen, unable to do anything, because I literally didn't know what to do."

- "I have yet to encounter a situation that presents me with any real challenge regarding execution. I simply don't allow myself to make mistakes."

- "I was scared I might fail, so I told everyone that I was going to fail so I wouldn't look like a fool if I did. But in the end it all worked out OK."

- "That describes every day at my last job. Things were constantly changing, and there was just no way to keep up with it all. What a mess. And when you consider that my manager was offering zero support and guidance, well, it's easy to understand why I had absolutely no idea what to do."

Positive signals: These types of answers can indicate a good fit with the organization's culture.

- "It really helps to have a close group of peers with whom you can discuss opportunities and share ideas. I actually initiated a forum of really talented people from all over the organization at my last job. I set it up so we met once a week to discuss our challenges and problems. It was a great way to get feedback and advice, especially when I wasn't sure how to do something."

- "I ask lots of questions, and if possible, I spread my queries out among many different people. Not only does this ensure I'm not a burden on any one person, it also allows me to get a lot of different perspectives."

- "I was honest with the customer and explained that I wasn't familiar with what he was looking for, but that I would connect him with the person in our company who was the expert on this. I made this connection within the 24-hour window I had promised to the customer, and I kept in touch with both the customer and our expert throughout the process. Then I went and learned as much about the issue as I could so next time I would be prepared."

- "A client said she simply couldn't wait for my solution, and that even though her company managers preferred to work with me, they had to go with a competitor who could offer an immediate solution. Up until then we'd been talking on the phone, so while I told her I understood, I asked if I could visit with them in person that afternoon to maybe gain a new perspective on the situation. After a review of their system that took less than an hour, I was able to find a solution, and the customer went with us."

- "I thought that the problem might be far more complex than the person making the request realized. So I called a team meeting to review the situation and to brainstorm how we might fix it. The feedback was great, and I left the meeting knowing exactly what to do. I used to think it took too long, and was too arduous a process, to bring everybody together like that. But I now realize the value of putting time in at the front of problem solving. It's much more productive than getting everyone together after the fact to clean up a mess that resulted from a hasty and poorly made decision."

Again, this is just an abbreviated example. Your list of Warning Signs and Positive Signals could be a page or more in length each. But this example demonstrates that the Positive Signals show what good answers sound like and Warning Signs represent what bad answers sound like. Too often interviewers let something slide, miss a key signal, or just misinterpret the answer. Your Answer Guidelines are designed to show exactly what good and bad answers sound like, so when you or your hiring managers hear either one, you can identify it immediately.

WHY DO WE USE ACTUAL ANSWERS?

While Leadership IQ is the only group I know of that has developed a formalized approach to creating Answer Guidelines, every once in awhile I do see somebody else attempt to assemble an interview question answer key. But instead of giving examples of actual answers, they give general admonitions such as "Look for answers that indicate adherence to ethical standards" or "Beware of answers that indicate a passive acceptance of accountability but no proactive assumption of accountability."

There's nothing inherently terrible about these guidelines, but they are pretty abstract, and that alone renders them woefully inadequate as teaching tools. I'm sure I'm not the only one who finds it challenging to learn in the abstract. For instance, say you were trying to teach me how to make a candidate more relaxed in an interview in order to get him to loosen up and drop his guard. You could tell me "Arrange the seating in the interview room so it puts the candidate at ease."

That advice is fine as long as my vision of what that looks like is similar to yours (and it probably isn't). Instead you want to say something less abstract, perhaps "Never sit across the desk from the candidate because that creates a barrier. Get out from behind the desk and arrange the chairs so they face each other. Then turn the chairs about 20 degrees away from each other. That will create a much more open and comfortable space, but it eliminates any chance of your knees hitting his."

The latter instruction is a lot more explicit and far more actionable. Similarly, when you use clips of actual answers in your Brown Shorts Answer Guidelines, it's a lot easier for folks to learn what good and bad answers sound like. You're not leaving anything open to misinterpretation as you do when you provide an abstract explanation.

Of course, a lot of the real candidate answers that your Brown Shorts questions elicit are going to be long-winded and contain irrelevant details. Also, the responses will vary wildly from candidate to candidate, and you can't plan for every possible permutation. But the snippets that appear in your Answer Guidelines don't need to contain or cover everything that could ever be said. You just need to represent the hallmarks (Positive Signals and Warning Signs) of the good and bad answers so both can be identified quickly and accurately while you're listening to all those specific situational details. The Answer

Guidelines ensure that you can accurately assess the content of the answers. Factors such as the length and specificity of a candidate's answers can be assessed independently.

Take a minute and carefully re-read the example list of Warning Signs and Positive Signals. Now that you've got a better understanding of how it all works, you should be able to pick out the defining characteristics of that organization's high and low performers. These Brown Shorts qualities are intimated everywhere in the snippets I shared.

MARK'S ASSESSMENT OF THE ANSWER GUIDELINES

At some point during our projects (at least the ones I'm personally involved with), I like to read through the client's Brown Shorts Answer Guidelines as though I were part of the culture and not an independent observer. It gives me a chance to react as their managers will likely react and anticipate how they'll feel when reading the Guidelines.

Following are some of my initial reactions to the sample set of Brown Shorts Answer Guidelines; I approached my review as though I were an executive at that chemical company. And based on what I know about this company (their culture), my comments reflect the thoughts that went through my head immediately after hearing that snippet of answer. Perhaps I got a little snarky or sarcastic, but I wanted to give you my relatively unfiltered perspective.

Remember that two of the Brown Shorts for this company were:

- You take ownership of problems—even if you're not the one who will ultimately fix it, you shepherd the process until it's resolved.
- You're a self-directed learner—you take full responsibility for growing and developing your skills, and while you may not learn everything, you're in a constant state of growth.

Here are my thoughts.

Warning Signs

These types of answers can indicate a poor fit with the organization's culture.

- "When you don't know how to do something you just placate the requestor and obfuscate the issue until hopefully it starts to go away. I've found it to be pretty common for a customer or boss who gets all hot and bothered over an issue to completely forget it within 72 hours."

Mark's comment: I'm sure glad my doctor doesn't talk like this. I guess you'd have to be writhing in pain for more than 72 hours before this person would finally decide to take ownership of your problem. This is major denial and the opposite of true accountability.

- "I had one boss who was terrible at communication, and a lot of times it negatively affected the procedures and work flow in our department. I know it really impacted my work and made my life pretty miserable. There were a lot of times when I didn't find out about process changes until after the fact. This slowed me up a lot, and I spent many days just frozen, unable to do anything, because I literally didn't know what to do."

Mark's comment: I'm concerned here about the way this person was "frozen" by a lack of clarity. First, everyone is going to suffer some poor communication, but does that mean we all freeze up because of it? Or do we actively seek out whatever information we can find and take some positive steps forward (as our Brown Shorts say we do)? Second, I'm concerned about the speed with which this person dumps all the responsibility for poor communication on the boss—again, not much ownership of the problem.

- "I have yet to encounter a situation that presents me with any real challenge regarding execution. I simply don't allow myself to make mistakes."

Mark's comment: Show me somebody who's never made a mistake and I'll show you somebody who's never had a job. How can you be a self-directed learner without a little humility that says "there are things I still need to learn?"

- "I was scared I might fail, so I told everyone that I was going to fail so I wouldn't look like a fool if I did. But in the end it all worked out OK."

Mark's comment: There is a fine line between self-deprecation (which can be endearing) and a lack of self-esteem (which is not). As noted in our Brown Shorts, I don't want people who are preparing to fail. I want people who take ownership for ensuring that things do *not* fail and who learn the necessary skills to guarantee that outcome.

- "That describes every day at my last job. Things were constantly changing, and there was just no way to keep up with it all. What a mess. And when you consider that my manager was offering zero support and guidance, well, it's easy to understand why I had absolutely no idea what to do."

Mark's comment: If this person was presented with opportunities for self-directed learning every day at his last job, and he described that situation as a "mess," it's pretty easy to see he isn't going to fit into our Brown Shorts. Plus, isn't it reasonable to think that after the first few hundred times you were asked to do something you didn't know how to do, that maybe, just maybe, you'd start to learn how to do a few of those things and solve the problem?

Positive Signals
These types of answers can indicate a good fit with the organization's culture.

- "It really helps to have a close group of peers with whom you can discuss opportunities and share ideas. I actually initiated a forum of really talented people from all over the organization at my last job. I set it up so we met once a week to discuss our challenges and problems. It was a great way to get feedback and advice, especially when I wasn't sure how to do something."

Mark's comment: This person took ownership of creating her own system for self-directed learning. That pretty much exemplifies our Brown Shorts.

- "I ask lots of questions, and if possible, I spread my queries out among many different people. Not only does this ensure I'm not a burden on any one person, it also allows me to get a lot of different perspectives."

Mark's comment: This shows ownership and learning, all in one sentence.

- "I was honest with the customer and explained that I wasn't familiar with what he was looking for, but that I would connect him with the person in our company who was the expert on this. I made this connection within the 24-hour window I had promised to the customer, and I kept in touch with both the customer and our expert throughout the process. Then I went and learned as much about the issue as I could so next time I would be prepared."

Mark's comment: This person took ownership for finding the customer a solution, even if he wasn't the one providing it. There is also a clear sign of ownership for making sure the customer was well served throughout the process. And then to put the cherry on top, he learned about the issue so that next time he'd be able to solve the issue by himself.

- "A client said she simply couldn't wait for my solution, and that even though her company managers preferred to work with me, they had to go with a competitor who could offer an immediate solution. Up until then we'd been talking on the phone, so while I told her I understood, I asked if I could visit with them in person that afternoon to maybe gain a new perspective on the situation. After a review of their system that took less than an hour, I was able to find a solution, and the customer went with us."

Mark's comment: It's amazing how taking ownership of a customer problem often leads to getting a lot more business from that customer. This person didn't get angry and tell the customer where to stick her account. The customer's needs were put first, but then, by taking full ownership of the problem, he didn't just let it go. He went back in to the customer, figured out the underlying issue, and won the account back.

- "I thought that the problem might be far more complex than the person making the request realized. So I called a team meeting to review the situation and to brainstorm how we might fix it. The feedback was great, and I left the meeting knowing exactly what to do. I used to think it took too long, and was too arduous a process, to bring everybody together like that. But I now realize the value of putting time in at the front of problem solving. It's much more productive than getting everyone together after the fact to clean up a mess that resulted from a hasty and poorly made decision."

Mark's comment: Self-directed learning doesn't just have to be specific knowledge or skills; it can also be knowledge about *how* to solve problems. And that's the growth that this person shows in her answer.

The Answer Guidelines bring your Brown Shorts to life. I said this before, but it bears repeating—learning things in the abstract is hard. I see many different companies that instruct their hiring managers and HR departments to look for people with integrity, positive attitude, influence, innovation, proactivity, achievement, and all the rest. But what do those things sound like when they are coming at me during an interview? Yes, I want proactive, positive people with integrity. But how do I know when I'm interviewing someone like that? How do I tell if this person, or that person, really has all those characteristics? Remember what I said in Chapter 1 about the need for Behavioral Specificity? The Answer Guidelines are all about Behavioral Specificity. If you don't bring your Brown Shorts to life with examples of actual answers, it may be impossible to accurately evaluate the people you interview.

Here's a nonworkplace example of what I mean. If my wife sends me to the store to buy new sheets and she says, "Get something that matches our bedroom," I'm dead. I think gold silk sheets would look good—you know, the kind that when I lie on them make me look like a Roman Emperor waiting to be fed grapes. So the instructions "Get something that matches . . ." is not nearly specific enough for me to meet my wife's expectations. I am going to need a more fleshed-out example, something like "The best colors to match our bedroom would be medium or dark shades of brown. No pastels and no white. Make sure they are pure organic cotton, and don't even look at anything that has a thread count of 300 or lower—400 and up is best. They should feel like cool silk to the touch, but whatever you do, don't get real silk (my wife knows me a little too well). Really busy patterns aren't going to work, and floral is out, so look for something uncomplicated, geometric, but still flowing, you know, like the Picasso you love so much at MoMA." Now *these* guidelines give me a good understanding of exactly what's good and what's bad. I'm going to be able to recognize the perfect sheets the second I lay eyes on them.

One final note before we move into the execution phase of your Answer Guidelines. Just by looking over the sample guideline shown previously, you can see that your hiring managers will need to familiarize themselves with the content in there. Don't worry—this doesn't take long. In fact, most people need to read through the guidelines only a few times to understand them completely. But your managers will need to practice using the guidelines in order to make the most efficient use of them. Remember the exercise at the beginning of this chapter where a group of managers couldn't agree on how to rate the answer I showed them? Well, after teaching the Answer Guidelines, we did a few more exercises like that. And the second time those managers rated the answers all within 1 point of each other, with most scores landing squarely on the same number. That's hiring consistency.

WHERE DO ANSWER GUIDELINES COME FROM?

Now that you have a feel for what Brown Shorts Answer Guidelines look like and how they work, I assume you're thinking "Sure, we can show pages of actual answer examples, but where do they come from?" Here's the answer, and it may surprise you a bit. Those answer examples, both good and bad, come from your current employees. That's right; those Positive Signals are your high performers being high performers. And those Warning Signs are coming straight from the minds of your lower performers.

I've yet to see an executive receive his Brown Shorts Answer Guidelines and not get at least a little wind knocked out of him. I've even heard a few respond with a comment like "Umm, these are our people—saying these things—that run totally counter to our Brown Shorts? How did this happen?" Of course, we know how it happened, but now we need to focus on moving forward.

So how are you supposed to get those unfiltered responses from your employees? The answer is, you ask. You ask cleverly, but basically, you ask. Here's the approach we take at Leadership IQ when an organization brings us in on a Brown Shorts project. First we discover the organization's Brown Shorts and then use that insight to craft its Brown Shorts Interview Questions. We then make a few strategic tweaks to the questions, after which we put them into an online survey. Finally, we send that survey to the organization's employees. Note that we typically use a carefully selected sample of employees, and we use a statistical method called a power study to determine how many respondents we'll need for the survey.

But even if you don't have access to these kinds of tools and resources, you can still conduct an effective employee survey to give you the information you need. In fact, your Brown Shorts Interview Questions are so powerful that you'll get some amazingly honest answers even if you don't make the tweaks. (I'll share more on what the tweaks are, and why you may want to consider making them, in just a bit.) Leadership IQ performs many employee surveys every year. As a result, we've collected piles of data on why some surveys generate better responses than others. One critical factor we've found relates to how the survey is framed. You don't want to just blast out a survey with five interview questions and ask people to respond. All that will do is make your current employees feel like they're re-interviewing for their jobs—not an effective use of anyone's time. (You have performance management systems to determine if someone should remain in a job.) Instead, you want employees to feel like they're helping the organization define and establish its standards (which they are).

Companies choose to work with an outside firm like Leadership IQ because when sensitive questions are asked, people feel more comfortable talking to an independent professional. (It's kind of the same as people telling their life stories to a bartender they've never met before.) It's confidential, it's secure, and there's no lingering weirdness after the conversation or fear that something they said will be used against them down the line. And, frankly, it's nice to have an outside perspective, because your company managers may not always be able to see what's right in front of them. We saw this example in the chemical company that did the question rating exercise at the start of this chapter. Even though those managers were living and breathing their Brown Shorts every day, they still struggled to articulate them clearly.

Let's look at this another way. I've lost 40 pounds in the past few years. Yet, when I look in the mirror, I still see pretty much the same body. That's because I look in the mirror every day, which makes it difficult to visually track the gradual physical changes that happen during weight loss. It's not until I take out some old pictures that I can see differences. My age now starts with the number 4, and yet, aside from the much more obvious gray streak in my hair, I don't think I look much older than when my age started with the number 2. OK, perhaps I'm delusional, but aren't we all? Just a little bit?

Whether it's our bodies or our organizational culture, surveying ourselves objectively is a challenge. And that's why outside groups like Leadership IQ can usually get more thorough results, especially with surveys that ask about sensitive topics. But again, you can certainly conduct this survey yourself and get the results you need. You just have to frame the survey properly.

WHAT'S IN THE SURVEY?

There are four steps to framing an effective survey. You need all four pieces, and they need to be executed in the following order.

Framing a Survey Step Number 1: An Invitation to Participate

First, invite people to participate in the survey. An invitation helps plant the seed that by completing the survey they're choosing to help the organization. You will lose the warm and fuzzy edge if you make the survey sound mandatory. Be sure to provide a few background details (keep it short), and to give simple instructions—you don't want to make this complicated and turn people off from participating.

Following are three actual e-mails sent by senior executives inviting their employees to participate in a Brown Shorts Answer Guidelines survey. They are all great models to emulate.

> **Example 1:** We have asked an outside firm, Leadership IQ, to help us understand how to better interview and hire people that more closely match our unique culture. They have started their work with a first stage of discussion,

and are on to the next stage. This is where we would like your help. Please take just a few minutes to complete the short and important survey at the link below and give them your thoughts. You will find it interesting, and I appreciate your support of our desire to learn how to do an even better job of "growing our team together." Please take time to give us your feedback before Monday, June 1st.

Example 2: I need your help. As you know, we're growing fast as a company, and it's time to grow our team to match. We've got a great recipe for success right now, and I want to make sure that every new hire we bring on board is a great fit for our culture. And who better to ask for help with that than the folks who embody that culture? With the contribution of just a few moments of your time to answer the five survey questions attached, you'll be making an impact on whom and how we hire. Don't worry about making it pretty or grammatically perfect. I'm far more interested in hearing your candid thoughts. Please email me your completed surveys by the end of the week.

Example 3: ACME Corp. has asked survey firm Leadership IQ to help research the attitudes and characteristics that make our organization so successful. And because you exemplify those successful characteristics, Leadership IQ is asking for your insights. The attached survey consists of six open-ended research questions. Please answer them based on your own beliefs and experiences. We want to know what you think about the characteristics that make people successful in this organization. And we also want to know about some situations in which you've personally evidenced those successful characteristics.

Framing a Survey Step Number 2: Warm-Up Questions

Begin the survey with a few easy questions about the characteristics that exemplify success and failure at your organization. These warm-up questions serve two purposes. First, they loosen people up and let them feel more fluid and competent about taking the survey. You never want the first question in a survey to feel like a hit to the head with a two-by-four; you want to ease people into the process. Second, these warm-up questions validate your Brown Shorts Discovery. The employee responses will confirm whether or not you really nailed down those Brown Shorts high and low performer characteristics.

Your warm-up questions might sound something like this:

- Please list three to five attitudes or personality traits that you think describe the *most* successful people at Company X.
- Please list three to five attitudes or personality traits that you think describe the *least* successful people at Company X.

Framing a Survey Step Number 3: Introduce Your Brown Shorts Questions

Once people are warmed up and feeling ready to share, you can introduce your Brown Shorts Interview Questions. As I've said, it's absolutely fine to go ahead and use them exactly as written, the same way you will in your interviews. But because you're not going to have the luxury of any follow-up or probing questions, it's a good idea to make a few tweaks to compensate for that. The goal is to gather as many real-life situations as possible, so consider each question and how you might, with a small tweak, better achieve that objective.

For example, say one of your Brown Shorts questions is "Could you tell me about the most difficult customer you dealt with?" Unlike in an interview, the survey is not intended to assess how forthcoming the person on the other end of this question will be about providing details that reveal attitude (why I earlier told you to delete your leading questions). In the survey, you want to make sure you get those details. So you might tweak your question to sound more like "Could you tell me about the two most difficult customers you dealt with?" By adding in the "two" you'll probably get at least two somewhat detailed descriptions of situations that involved difficult customers. This maximizes the time you've got with your respondents, and it ensures that you're going to get the information you need.

We always make a second important tweak. In addition to asking about personal examples, we also ask survey participants to describe what they've seen others do in these situations. For example, consider the Brown Shorts question "Could you tell me about the two most difficult customers you dealt with?" Here, instead of just asking about their individual experiences with difficult customers, you might also ask them to describe any situations they may have observed where a peer struggled to deal with a difficult customer.

Note here that bringing in the "other party" option is a great way to make people feel safe to share. When you were a teenager, did you ever want to ask your parents something really important but, because it was a sensitive topic, you were afraid how they would react? If you ever faced that situation, then you probably began your question with "I have a friend . . . (who was offered drugs, who saw someone cheating, or who whatever)." It's the biggest parenting joke around because we all know who the "friend" really is. But it's a useful device because it allows the teenager to raise sensitive topics that might otherwise have remained unspoken.

The same rule applies here when we ask employees to describe situations in which their colleagues have struggled or faced difficult customers. It allows us to assess the extent to which their personal answers have the same intensity and directionality as the answers about their colleagues. And thus we can more accurately evaluate their responses and build better scoring ranges.

Framing a Survey Step Number 4: Analyze

The final step involves analyzing these dozens, or hundreds, or thousands, of survey responses. All you've done so far is gather data; you haven't actually built any Answer Guidelines. So now you've got to code and analyze every survey response, grade it, identify whether it represents a positive or negative example, and rate the degree to which it's positive or negative. Once that's all accomplished, you can select the best snippets for examples to use in your Brown Shorts Answer Guidelines. At Leadership IQ we also subject all the responses to some pretty advanced textual analysis (some of which I'll share in the next chapter) that identifies the specific themes in the responses, as well as various types of language uses, grammar, verb tenses, emotional language, and much more.

Implementing the survey may get a bit technical, but the underlying idea is quite simple: you're testing your Brown Shorts Interview Questions and asking employees to tell you what good and bad answers sound like. If you do that, you'll have great questions, and you'll know how to identify the great (and not great) answers. You'll significantly increase the odds of picking out the future high performers and avoiding the low performers.

For free downloadable resources including the latest research, discussion guides, and forms please visit www.leadershipiq.com/hiring.

5

Scoring the Answers

You've got your Brown Shorts Answer Guidelines, and with this you can accurately diagnose who's likely to succeed, or fail, in your unique organizational culture. But you still need to know how to rate your candidates' answers against your Answer Guidelines. Let's start simply, with the form and scale you'll be using to grade the interview responses. Here's how it works.

First, it's a good idea to have an actual rating form. Table 5.1, versions of which you can download and edit at www.leader shipiq.com/hiring, is our suggested starting point.

Table 5.1. Score Your Candidates

Candidate Name:

Position Interviewing For:

Scores on Skills Tests: Scoring Scale (Pass/Fail)

Mandatory Hiring Tests: Drug Screen, Credit Check: Scoring Scale (Pass/Fail)

Brown Shorts Characteristic 1:	Poor Fit					Great Fit	
	1	2	3	4	5	6	7
Brown Shorts Characteristic 2:	Poor Fit					Great Fit	
	1	2	3	4	5	6	7
Brown Shorts Characteristic 3:	Poor Fit					Great Fit	
	1	2	3	4	5	6	7
Brown Shorts Characteristic 4:	Poor Fit					Great Fit	
	1	2	3	4	5	6	7
Brown Shorts Characteristic 5:	Poor Fit					Great Fit	
	1	2	3	4	5	6	7

You may already have some kind of form or automated talent management system that you use to record the results of a candidate's skills tests and drug screens. If so, it's often possible to merge the Brown Shorts rating with these other forms or systems. This doesn't have to be fancy, and it shouldn't be complicated or difficult to use. The goal is to have a reliable and consistent way to capture your Brown Shorts analysis so you can make an effective and objective comparison of your candidates.

WHY DO WE USE A SEVEN-POINT SCALE?

Nonresearchers often look at our rating scale and say, "Huh? Why the seven-point scale? And why are only numbers 1 and 7 labeled?" Without getting overly statistical here (although I'd love to because bad survey scales are a pet peeve of mine), the answer is that seven-point scales provide better data. Figure 5.1, which is a repeat of Figure 4.1 shown here for your convenience, is again an example of our seven-point scale.

There are several reasons why this is the case. First, if you use a narrower scale (like 3 or 5 points), the data usually skew to the side with the higher scores. People typically don't like checking any box that implies "this person is terrible," and interviewers are no different. It feels judgmental to make such a serious determination about someone, especially when you've only just met the person. And lots of interviewers wrongly believe that nice people don't give critical ratings. So the tendency is to give higher scores

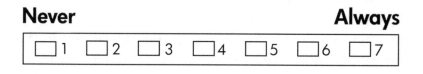

Figure 5.1. The Seven-Point Scale

than are actually warranted to somehow show "I'm a good and nice person, and I don't judge other people harshly."

The danger in this kind of behavior should be obvious, but the fact remains that this behavior exists. Using a broader scale balances out the impact of this expected (and understandable) behavior. Interviewers can then give a lower score (like 2 or 3 or 4) without feeling too bad about it.

The next rationale for using a seven-point scale is that you don't want to label every number on the scale. The endpoints in Figure 5.1 are clearly labeled with 1 indicating Never and 7 indicating Always. However, we purposely leave the numbers 2 through 6 empty of any description. We find that it's too easy for people to have different interpretations of the words on a scale, or to feel that the actual distance between the words isn't equal. This messes up the scores. Even worse, more description prevents people from giving certain scores; people often won't give a 1 or 2 because they think the labels are too harsh or too far away from a 3. So our scale has been carefully designed to encourage people to use the full range from 1 to 7 and to not shy away from giving scores on the lower end. This is important because rating inflation presents a very real danger.

As an aside here, one of the many interesting findings from Leadership IQ's Global Talent Management Survey is that executives see a significant discrepancy between the number of high performers they actually have and the number of people to whom they're giving top ratings on annual performance reviews. In other words, there are far fewer high performers than the scores would lead you to believe. As I said previously, rating inflation is a major issue.

You'll notice that I haven't mentioned even-numbered scales like four- or ten-point scales. Again, sparing you the math, a rating scale needs to have a middle: a point equidistant between both endpoints. And the last time I checked, 2.5 and 5.5 don't actually appear on most even-numbered scales. I don't mean to use this space as a marketing push for my book *Hundred Percenters*, but if you happen to have a copy of it available, you'll see a big chunk of the Appendix is devoted to explaining why seven-point scales are the most effective. Check it out if this is a subject you want to know more about. Or visit www.leadershipiq.com and read my articles on survey and scale design.

WHAT CONSTITUTES A LOW SCORE?

I hear this question a lot from the folks participating in the certification process for Hiring for Attitude. Unfortunately, the most accurate answer is "It depends." It depends on your talent pool, your Brown Shorts, what you're hiring for, and more. And those are just some of the factors we analyze when we develop standards for our clients. Plus, we take a few candidate pools and statistically analyze the spread of scores to see where the various thresholds occur. But that all takes some work, and I realize that you're reading this book because you want an actual answer right this minute—so here it is.

First, you need a range that unequivocally indicates when a candidate is immediately out of consideration. Typically, this is represented by a score of 1 to 3. If you get even one response that rates a 1 to 3, the candidate isn't a fit for one (or more) of your Brown Shorts. And it's a clear indication that this person shares at least one (and maybe more) big characteristic with your low performers (a good sign this might be a Talented Terror). A score of 1 to 3 is all you need to know. Discussing it further isn't going to make that person magically turn into a good cultural fit; it's just going to deplete your mental energy. We're not talking about the difference between a 6 and a 7 here; we're talking about the 1, 2, and 3 scores. So if that's the score, immediately dismiss the candidate from your consideration.

Since this is so important, let's review. When you're scoring a candidate's responses to your Brown Shorts Interview Questions, even one score of a 1, 2, or 3 should eliminate that candidate from consideration. And if you're really serious about talent management for your whole company, you should remove that candidate from consideration for your other positions as well. If you're a good interviewer and you know someone does not fit your company's Brown Shorts, do you really want another manager to hire that person and cause problems for other people? Sure, your area avoided this mistake, but what about those other departments?

TALLYING THE SCORES

Assuming that the candidate clears this hurdle and successfully completes the full interview, all you need to do next is average all the scores together. From there, it's simple: the candidate with the highest score should be your first choice (assuming that person passes all your other hiring tests).

But highest scores notwithstanding, I'd be concerned if your best scores are in the 4 to 5 range. You really want to see your best candidates rating a final 6-point-something or even a 7. So if you're finding that most candidates are mediocre fits—not awful, but not great—it's a sign that there's probably something broken in your recruiting process (I'll cover that in Chapter 6).

Another question we hear a lot during certification training is "What if there are several of us doing the interviews and our scores vary?" Well, right now, with your current system, your evaluations probably do vary. That's why we have the Brown Shorts Answer Guidelines. You already conducted the analysis about what constitutes good and bad answers. That's your guide. Any discrepancies after the interview should immediately be brought back to that guide for the final resolution. Your Answer Guidelines hold the answers about who will, and won't, succeed.

WHAT ARE WE ACTUALLY RATING?

This is the single biggest question I am asked, and it's also the most exciting to answer. (I know that *exciting* is a relative term, but come on, say it with me: "Ain't no party like a Brown Shorts party 'cause a Brown Shorts party don't stop!") First, you're evaluating the extent to which the candidate reflects your Brown Shorts. For example, say that yours is a highly social culture where the best employees enjoy working on teams and sharing credit. So you might ask a Brown Shorts Interview Question such as "Could you tell me about a time when working on a team was challenging?" You'll get a response that you'll then compare to the sample answers in your Brown Shorts Answer Guidelines. This will let you accurately assess if what the candidate revealed about his or her attitude regarding teams reflected any of the same attitudes about teamwork provided by your current high and low performers.

On the surface, it's an easily understood process, but there can be a bit more subtlety. For instance, what if the candidate generally seems to share your Brown Shorts, but his answers are kind of vague? Or pretty short? Or rambling? Or anything less than a crisp, clear, factual, and personal answer recounting specific experiences? Well, now we're not just rating the extent to which the candidate's answer fits with our Brown Shorts— we're also looking at the credibility and delivery of his answer. Two different candidates can both say "Yes, I have lots of team experiences," but one of them could deliver the answer with lots of specifics and the other with empty platitudes. Thus, one of those candidates will get high marks—he can prove his Brown Shorts—and the other, while seemingly in sync with your Brown Shorts, doesn't have the specifics to back it up.

TEXTUAL ANALYSIS

Here is where the really exciting stuff comes in. Leadership IQ has been engaged in some cutting-edge textual analysis research to assess the differences in language usage between high and low performers. That is, we know things like whether high performers primarily use the past or future tense in their answers, what kinds of pronouns and adverbs low performers choose, and so much more. This is the "rocket science" of our industry, and I have never seen any other group get even close to the level of our research.

So let me share with you some of our "Holy Cow!" findings. We know what constitutes a good answer and what constitutes a bad answer; that's why we have our Answer Guidelines. So we analyzed the language style and grammar across tens of thousands of Answer Guidelines responses and compared them to see how high and low performer answers varied. The statistics I'm going to share are rounded to the nearest 5 percent. I did this because we're always adding more data into our analyses and these numbers may change. And given the long life span of books, you may be reading this one years after the initial printing, which means there could be more current data. Certainly use the following numbers to get started, but also go to www .leadershipiq.com/hiring for the latest statistics.

Our textual analysis focused on five categories: pronouns, tense, voice, emotions, and qualifiers. Here are the results.

Pronouns
First person pronouns: The high performer answers (Positive Signal category) contain roughly 60 percent more first person pronouns (I, me, we) than answers given by the low performers (Warning Signs category).

Second person pronouns: Low performer answers contain about 400 percent more second person pronouns (you, your) than high performer answers.

Third person pronouns: Low performer answers use about 90 percent more third person pronouns (he, she, they) than high performer answers.

Neuter pronouns: Low performer answers use 70 percent more neuter pronouns (it, itself) than high performer answers.

So what does all this mean? Simply put, high performers talk about themselves and what they did. In contrast, typical low performer answers contained a lot more second and third person language. High performers might say something like "I called the customers on Tuesday and I asked them to share their concerns." A low performer might say "Customers need to be contacted so they can express themselves . . ." or "You should always call customers and ask them to share their concerns."

High performers talk about themselves and how they've used their great attitudes because they have lots of great experiences to draw from. They don't shy away from using first person pronouns. But low performers don't have those great attitudinal experiences and are thus more likely to give abstract answers that merely describe how "you" should handle it. This is really nothing more than a hypothetical response; it doesn't show what that person actually did in this situation. Additionally, research has found that when people lie, they often use more second and third person pronouns because they're subconsciously disassociating themselves from the lie.

The lesson here is to listen carefully to whether people are talking about "I/me"—which is good—or if they're talking about "you/he/it"—which is not so good. Figure 5.2 illustrates this serious concept in a more humorous manner.

Verb Tense

Past tense: Answers from high performers use 40 percent more past tense than answers from low performers.

Present tense: Answers from low performers use 120 percent more present tense than answers from high performers.

Future tense: Answers from low performers use 70 percent more future tense than answers from high performers.

Figure 5.2. Low Performers vs. High Performers

In a nutshell, when you ask high performers to tell you about a past experience, they will actually tell you about that past experience. And, quite logically, they will use the past tense. By contrast, low performers will answer your request to describe a past experience with lots of wonderfully spun tales about what they are (present tense) doing, or what they will (future tense) do. Unlike high performers, they can't tell you about all those past experiences because they don't have them.

So, for instance, when asked to describe a difficult customer situation, high performers will respond with an example stated in the past tense. "I had a customer who was having issues with her server and was about to miss her deadline." In contrast, low performers are more likely to express their response in the present or future tense. "When a customer is upset, the number one rule is to never admit you don't know the answer" or "I would calm an irrational person by making it clear I know more than she does."

You'll also notice that those present and future tenses are usually accompanied by second and third person pronouns ("you/he/she/they did"), whereas the past tense is linked to the first person pronoun ("I/me/we did . . .").

Voice

Answers in the Warning Signs category use 40 to 50 percent more passive voice than the answers in the Positive Signal category. OK, this one probably requires a little explanation. To keep things simple, let's talk about active and passive voice.

> **Active voice:** In the active voice, the subject of the sentence is doing the action, for example, "Bob likes the CEO." Bob is the subject, and he is doing the action—he likes the boss, the object of the sentence. Another example is "I heard it through the grapevine." In this case, *I* is the subject, the one who is doing the action. *I* is hearing it, which is the object of the sentence.
>
> **Passive voice:** In the passive voice, the target of the action gets promoted to the subject position. Instead of saying "Bob likes the CEO," the passive voice says "The CEO

is liked by Bob." The subject of the sentence becomes the CEO, but she isn't doing anything. Rather, she is just the recipient of Bob's liking. The focus of the sentence has changed from Bob to the CEO. For the other example, we'd say "It was heard by me through the grapevine."

Notice how much more stilted the passive voice sounds. It is awkward and appears affected, meaning it's often used by people trying to sound smarter than they actually are. To be sure, there are academic types who rely more on the passive voice, and academe has higher concentrations of this rhetorical style. But more often than not, intelligent people will speak directly, with the active voice. Parenthetically, this lesson should be applied to your writing. Great writers spend most of their time in the active voice. And that's where your next big memo or report should live.

This issue is not a deal breaker, and in fact, in the sciences, using passive voice might be a Brown Shorts characteristic. But be on the lookout for people who use the passive voice as an affectation to appear smarter than they are. And remember, the answers in the Warning Signs category use this particular style a lot more than the ones in the Positive Signal category.

Emotions

Positive emotions: High performer answers contain about 25 percent more positive emotions (happy, thrilled, excited) than low performer answers.

Negative emotions: Low performer answers contain about 90 percent more negative emotions (angry, afraid, jilted, pessimistic) than high performer answers.

The emotional issue is fairly easy to understand. High performers do talk about being excited more than low performers. However, the real difference with emotion is how infrequently high performers express negative emotions compared to low performers. In all of our research, we've seen that high performers don't get quite as angry as lower performers. It's not that they don't get mad and frustrated—they do (and it's often brought on by low performers). But high performers have more constructive outlets for doing something about these negative emotions. Given all their positive personality attributes, they don't get quite as viscerally worked up. And because they don't get as wound up, they're much more in control of those feelings and less likely to express them in an interview.

Qualifiers

Qualifiers is a broad category that covers anything that modifies, limits, hedges, or restricts the meaning of the answer. This list includes adverbs, negation, waffling, and absolutes.

> **Adverbs:** Answers in the low performer category contain 40 percent more adverbs (think of words ending in -ly, like *quickly, totally, thoroughly*) than the high performer answers.

High performers are far more likely to give answers without qualifiers. Their answers are direct, factual, in the past tense, and personal. Low performers, on the other hand, are more likely to qualify their answers. For instance, they might use adverbs to amp up their answers because the facts probably don't speak well enough on their own. So instead of listing a situation where they had a brilliant idea, they might say "I was constantly/always/often/usually (all adverbs) coming up with great ideas."

> **Negation:** Low performer answers use 130 percent more negation (no, neither) than high performer answers.

Partly due to a more negative predisposition and partly from a need to qualify their statements, low performer answers contain more negations. It's not uncommon (note the negation there) to hear low performers say things like "I had no idea what to do" or "Nobody in my department really knew what her or she was doing."

> **Waffling:** Low performers use 40 percent more waffling (could be, maybe, perhaps) than high performers.
> **Absolutes:** Low performers use 100 percent more absolutes (always, never) than high performers.

It may seem strange that waffling and absolutes would go hand in hand, but they do. Both tend to stem from insecurity. "Maybe I was on a team like that . . ." would be a pretty obvious hedge—the speaker obviously does not want to be pinned down. But the use of absolutes—"the people in this department never know what they're doing and always ask for my help"— also stems from insecurity and a need to show off. It also shows a tendency toward black-and-white thinking and a lack of intellectual flexibility, which are hardly great qualities.

We can listen to candidates' language and start to get a good feel about whether they're headed toward the high or low performer camps. Textual analysis is truly a revolutionary idea, and we're just scratching the surface of its many applications.

WHEN DO YOU DO THE SCORING?

So, all this analysis and rating is fantastic. But when do we do this awesome analysis? The short answer is that you want to evaluate your candidate as close to the actual time of the interview as possible. This can be tough to do real time, such as while the candidate is still talking, but you should aim for as soon as possible after the interview. Take a cue from clinical psychologists who often have 50-minute hours. They do therapy with the patient for 50 minutes and then spend the next 10 minutes finishing their notes. They capture their thoughts while they're still fresh and accurate. Otherwise, if you wait too long, you may forget important points. Wait too long, and certain biases creep in, your memory gets fuzzy, and you start confusing candidates.

In fact, two really bad circumstances can happen if you don't do your interview ratings immediately after the interview. First, your standards change. And more specifically, your standards start to loosen. It's not because you want them too, but the longer your hiring process takes, and the more candidates you interview, the more tired of the process you'll become.

I do this stuff professionally, and even I have occasionally thought, "Jeez-Louise, can't we find anybody that fits? How about we just take the next person with a pulse that walks in the door?" And if you really need to fill this position (for example, because you, as the manager, are doing all the work yourself), then you may become a little desperate. You might start to believe that a warm body is better than no body. Oh, you'll pay for that idea in a few months, but it just sounds so perfect when you're frustrated by your flippin' high standards eliminating all those possible candidates. This is why it's critical to conduct your evaluations immediately after the interview. You don't want to start thinking globally about your need to fill this position; instead, all you're thinking about this one person who was just sitting in your office. That's it. Don't sweat the big stuff—just focus on this one individual.

The second big problem with waiting too long to evaluate the interview is that the candidate becomes a memory—you forget who's who. When you conduct your evaluation immediately after the interview, you never have to go back and reevaluate each candidate. You did your evaluation. It's done. It is the most accurate it's going to be, and if you try to go back and redo the scores, those biases I mentioned start to come back full force.

BE SURE TO LISTEN

Finally, you need to listen. I mean really listen—no talking, no interjecting. Zipped lips work well. Here's a good technique. Whenever you get the urge to interject, bite your tongue and slowly count to three—one one thousand, two one thousand, three one thousand—keeping your mouth shut. The ensuing stretch of silence tends to make people uncomfortable, especially when they're being interviewed. They start thinking it's their fault no one is talking and say things to fill the void for fear of looking bad. In fact, when faced with an uncomfortable silence, people will start talking 95 percent of the time. You risk feeling a millisecond of discomfort, but it's worth it if it elicits the facts you are looking for.

Here's what an HR Generalist at the University of Washington-Tacoma shared with me regarding her experiences in Hiring for Attitude.

Once we dropped all our leading and hypothetical questions and just asked the Brown Shorts questions, I noticed something really interesting. A surprising number of interviewees didn't naturally give us too many details about the challenging scenarios that the Brown Shorts questions presented them with.

There was definitely a learning curve on the part of our hiring committee to allow that disconnect to happen. But that's only because the natural impulse is to jump in there and help the candidate with a follow-up question like "What was the outcome?" or "How did you deal with it?" But the key word here is *help*, and I had to remind our interviewers that we aren't there to help the candidates turn themselves into problem solvers (or whatever Brown Shorts we are looking for) when they weren't. Rather, we're there to find out if they already were problem solvers or not.

It took making a slight adjustment in our thinking, but now we all agree that we get far more honest answers when we don't ask the candidate to "tell me what I want to hear." So now when we ask a Brown Shorts Interview Question, and the candidate can't offer up a real-life situation where this happened to him or her, it tells us that this individual likely doesn't possess the Brown Shorts characteristics that we critically need.

As for the candidates who do give us detailed information, having our Brown Shorts Answer Guidelines has made us so much more prepared when making our hiring decisions. The

Answer Guidelines allow us to be objective and get all our interviewers on the same page when rating candidates. Typically the people we interview are really different, and the interview committee members already have a gut feeling after interacting with them. But having those Answer Guidelines down on paper makes our hiring decision that much more defensible. We know we did not hire on a hunch; we knew what was critical for the position, and that is what we hired for.

MORE ANSWER GUIDELINES EXAMPLES

I'll close this chapter by leaving you with some more snippets from a real-life Brown Shorts Answer Guidelines. It should be easy to identify this organization's Brown Shorts from their list of Warning Signs and Positive Signals. And make sure to pay attention to the pronouns, tense, voice, emotions, and qualifiers used. What do they all tell you about the candidate?

Brown Shorts Interview Question: Could you tell me about a time when you had to think outside the box?

Warning Signs: These types of answers can indicate a poor fit with the organization's culture.

- "I've never had a challenge I couldn't beat. At my last job I was the 'go-to' person when we needed innovative new ideas. Of course, my boss wasn't always my greatest supporter; he felt some of my ideas challenged company policy. But the customers sure liked that I was able to find ways to, you know, sorta dodge the rules and give them what they wanted. Shoot, I even

had some customers who would call me at home in the
evenings or on weekends to talk about what we might
be able to do. And I never minded taking those calls.
For me, my job always comes first. I sure moved a lot of
product at that company. I bet they miss me."

- "I only had to make the mistake once of stepping into
  a skill set that was unknown territory to figure out that
  being too innovative isn't a great thing. Besides, what
  I've found is that the demands for that kind of outside
  the box thinking usually only happen when somebody
  else messes up and puts us in an emergency situation.
  All I ever heard my last boss say was how important
  personal accountability was. He was like a broken
  record about it. So shouldn't that mean that the person
  who made the mess is the person who cleans up the
  mess?"

- "Any kind of opportunity to stretch my brain and really
  prove my value to the organization interests me. At
  my last job I was recognized for several of my original
  ideas. Perhaps you noticed that I listed some of them
  on my résumé? There should be one more award listed
  there, but I lost it due to bad office politics. But yeah,
  I'm great at out of the box thinking."

- "Right, my team wasn't really involved with that level
  of thinking, but I might have an example that applies.
  It was just really difficult at my last job for anyone to
  get an idea under management's radar. And that kind of
  killed any incentive for innovative thinking, you know
  what I mean? But I'm sure if I were given the challenge
  in a different kind of environment, I would come up
  with something really clever."

- "So, the customer seemed pretty happy with my solution. Of course, management was another issue, but that's just the way they were. But it's a lot more of a hands-off and open environment here though, isn't it? I mean, I would have a lot of space to kind of do my own thing, right?"

- "So when I couldn't get anyone to go with my idea, I admit, I dramatized the situation a bit to make the need for my idea appear a little more attractive in everyone's eyes. But it worked. People started listening to what I had to say, and we went with my idea. In the end there were really only a few people who were really unhappy about that. But they were the kind of people who are never happy about anything. But you definitely don't want me to get started on that . . . or do you want to hear about it?

Positive Signals: These types of answers can indicate a good fit with the organization's culture.

- "First, I checked in with the customer to make sure my idea would meet expectations. And that was a good call because I found that I did have to make a few changes. Then I had to consider just whom I could pull from each department to put together a great team to execute my idea. I didn't want to leave any one department vulnerable, because I knew this was going to take at least a week of concentrated effort from the entire team. But at the same time, I wanted to make sure I got the best people so as to meet, and ideally even surpass, the commitment I had made to the customer."

- "I didn't hesitate to ask around and gather as much feedback from my peers as I could get. Not that I put the burden on anyone else to come up with my answer for me, but I am extremely aware of the value of being open to other people's ideas."
- "With my idea, I was able to satisfy the customer's needs and end the conflict. But I also resolved an ongoing communication issue, which I discovered was originating from my organization. I actually found out that we had a history of these kinds of communication problems that typically led to some other kind of problem. I had to play investigator and really get in there and break the process down to see where the disconnect was taking place. And then, of course, before I approached my boss with the problem, I came up with a few solutions to rectify the problem. That was six years ago, and as far as I know, it was the last time anything like that happened. And I know if you ask my supervisor at that job, he'll tell you it's because of the changes I suggested. Not that I necessarily need the credit for that, but I do feel really proud of being an integral part of that change."
- "It required a lot of courage for me to stand behind my idea. But I was able to do it because I was confident that I had covered all my bases and that this was the very best solution for both the organization and the client. Win-wins are always good in my book."
- "It was really pretty thrilling because I had never faced a quality control challenge of that magnitude before. But then it got even better when my idea resulted in increased revenue to the company and solidified the

relationship with that customer. It was one of those days when I left work and my head was just floating in the clouds. I love those kinds of days."

- "I just could not get the customer to bite via any of the usual channels. But there was no way I was going to give up, because I knew we could make him happy. So I got permission to take one of their products home for the weekend, and I created a prototype of what it would look like if they were using the program I had suggested. Well, the customer loved it as soon as he saw it. He didn't even need to hear how much time and money it would save his company. Though, of course, I had prepared a full report that I shared with him. It was a really cool experience, and I really liked working with that customer. But then, all our customers were great to work with."

For free downloadable resources including the latest research, discussion guides, and forms please visit www.leadershipiq.com/hiring.

6

Recruiting for Your Brown Shorts

Collectively, we're doing a lousy job of attracting great talent. That's tough to hear, especially since it happens to be true. But I didn't say it first; you did—via the collective voice of your peers. While I've been writing this book, Leadership IQ has been conducting one of the largest talent-management studies ever done. We're looking at executives from more than 1,000 companies, folks strategically selected to represent every company size, every industry, and every major country. Our goal is to learn what's working—and what's not working—across the full talent-management continuum (recruiting, hiring, developing, engaging, leading, and retaining). It's a massive undertaking that's already presented us with tremendous amounts of information. And one thing that's coming through loud and clear is that the current trends in recruiting are definitely not working.

We asked the executives participating in the study to evaluate their companies' talent pipelines. And we asked them to consider in particular how successful they were in sourcing the following four categories of talent: executive, professional, technical, and unskilled. We received poor feedback, and this is what I mean by that. For each of the four talent categories, fewer than 10 percent of the companies said they were doing an excellent job at sourcing that talent. Plus, at least 65 percent of the companies said they were average or below average in sourcing talent in each of the four categories. Though these numbers show little overall success, we were able to observe that companies do the best job at sourcing professional employees, followed by technical employees, then executive employees, and finally unskilled employees. (The most up-to-date data on this study can be found at www.leadershipiq.com/hiring.)

Now some people look at that 65 percent for average or below average and say, "Well, I could live with being average—it's better than totally stinking." And to some extent that's true; technically speaking, being average is better than totally stinking. But average isn't good enough to get the talent you're after. This is an issue I see so many organizations getting wrong that it's worth taking a closer look at.

I don't care if you're hiring a housekeeper, an engineer, a nurse, or your next CEO, you want somebody in that role who "gets it"—who wants to be great at whatever the job entails. I didn't title this book *Lowered Expectations: A Guide to Hiring People That Aren't Totally Awful* for a reason. This book is about hiring high performers, the people who have the right skills and the right attitude to succeed at your organization. But the people you want to bring to your organization, the ones who are going to knock at your door and say, "Hey, look at me, I'm happy to wear your Brown Shorts and I want to work for you," aren't so easy to reach.

High performers aren't looking for an average job opportunity, a place to go five days a week just to kill some time and get a paycheck. They want more than that; they want ongoing success. They want a job where the culture fits their personality and where the clear path in front of them leads to being a high performer. But these great people aren't just sitting around waiting for your call. Generally, they're employed someplace else. Or even if they are in a career transition, you can bet they are going to choose their next job very carefully and not just jump at the first place that offers a steady paycheck.

Oh, you might get lucky and find that your next high performer is in a weakened negotiating position. Maybe he's been out of work for a while or is just entering the workforce. Or maybe you found a true diamond in the rough whom nobody else has discovered yet. But I wouldn't make hope or luck the foundation of your talent strategy.

Thinking competitively is a fairly typical and, for the most part, accepted mind-set in the sales world. You have competitors and those competitors have customers that you will most certainly try to steal away. You'll identify those customers, try to find where they're hurting, figure out how to solve that pain, understand what drives their purchasing, hone your pitch, highlight your advantages, and call, call, call. Welcome to Sales 101.

We understand and even celebrate this need for competitive differentiation and pursuit in the world of sales. But when it comes to sourcing talent, we often operate as though millions of high performers are sitting around with nothing better to do than jump at our job ads. We act as if all we have to do is describe our open positions and, voilà, the best of the best will line up outside our door.

The following example illustrates how great we are at selling ourselves in the sales world (and by "ourselves" I mean our companies), and what a lousy job we do of selling ourselves when it comes to sourcing talent. Imagine you're the CEO of a software company that makes video games, and you've just released a new game called *HurtsSoGood*.

When you announce *HurtsSoGood* to the marketplace, and the gamers at your press conference ask why they should buy your game, you of course have a strong pitch, maybe something like this:

> Aren't you frustrated with your current video games that aren't photorealistic, load too slowly, run too slowly, and don't inflict actual pain? Don't you want to play in the game instead of playing near the game? Isn't that why you abandon games after an average of only two weeks? I know I want a real rush from my games, and I'm sure you do too. *HurtsSoGood* solves all that with lifelike graphics, loading speeds under two seconds and running speeds even faster, and each copy comes with a set of hospital-quality electrodes that attach to your temples so whenever your character gets shot, you feel the actual pain. This is how warriors become warriors! So get off your feet, plant your butt on that couch, and become a warrior!

OK, so maybe that's not your exact response, but whatever your pitch sounds like, it's going to be compelling. You'll give a great answer that sells. You'll highlight the frustrations gamers feel with their current games, paint a vivid picture of why your game solves all those frustrations, and show folks how quickly they'll be enthralled with this game—shooting and getting shocked and whatever else. Everyone who hears your pitch will be awestruck.

Now, still imaging yourself as CEO of this software company, let's turn to your job ads—after all, you're going to need some pretty top-notch programmers with a great deal of moral flexibility to keep products like these coming. Based on reviews of thousands of real-world job ads, I distilled the data to find the average ad showing what your job ad probably looks like.

If you are a C++ Engineer with great math skills and experience developing video games, please read on!

What you need for this position:

- C++ Expertise
- Object-Oriented Design
- Foundation in Game Programming
- Strong Debugging Skills
- Strong 3D Graphics Skills (Open GL or Direct 3D)
- Foundation in Mathematics (vector, discrete)
- Experience in Developing with Version Control

What's in it for you:

Competitive salary and benefits, flexibility to work with multiple languages of your preference, sunny warm weather, and free lunches. So if you have heavy C/C++ experience, please apply today!

Wow, what happened? Your sales pitch to get people to buy the game was so compelling. I want to buy that game because you tapped into my current frustrations with all my other games (lousy graphics, too slow, no physical pain). You painted such a vivid picture of how the new game will make me feel like a warrior that I must have it now! I'm pumped up just thinking about it. But your pitch to get me to apply for the job offered none of that. The ad tells me what skills I should have, but why should I apply? The best benefits offered are competitive salary and free lunch? Seriously?

Why didn't all that great sales energy make it into the job ad? Most job ads sound more like the instruction manual to a VCR (oops, sorry, I mean a Blu-Ray player) than they do a compelling sales pitch. And that's a problem—the high performers you want all have better opportunities. They're not sitting around waiting for you to post some ineffectual job ad. In fact, they're not even going to notice that job ad. Most people who are going to notice that ad (and who will likely respond to it, thereby taking up your valuable time) are the folks you don't want—the people sitting around, reading generic job ads, and responding to any and all with an e-mail blast of their résumé. And believe me, there's a bad attitude story lurking behind almost every one of those candidates.

The high performers you're trying to recruit to make (or sell, or conceptualize) your products are as challenging to attract as are the customers you want to buy those products. So to get the candidates you want, you've got to put the same marketing effort into selling the "product" (in this case, the job and your organization) as you do when you market your products to the customers you want. And yet, when you look at most job ads (and really, recruiting pitches in any media look pretty similar), there are a lot more words devoted to "this is what we require for you to work here" than there are words about "this is why you're going to love working here." And even worse, all those requirements you list sound just like the requirements every other company lists. There's nothing to set you apart, to grab the attention of the right high performers so they stop and say, "Wow, this job sounds like something that might be even better than where I am right now. I should check it out."

Please note that I'm using the "job ads" in this chapter as a proxy for the overall recruiting message. Also, the job ad is the place in the recruiting chain where you typically have the greatest control over both the message and the delivery. If you can't get the message right in your ad or job post, you're definitely not going to get it right anywhere else (like job fairs and social media).

So unless you want to remain trapped in a world where fewer than 10 percent of leaders have excellent talent pipelines, you're going to have to change the way you recruit for the talent you want. The good news is that with all our research, we've distilled the probability of attracting high performers to apply for jobs at your company into this very simple formula. (See Figure 6.1.)

| P **P**robability of high performers applying to your company | = A **A**ttraction they feel to your organization's Brown Shorts | + U **U**rgency they feel to leave their current situation | – S **S**uspicions they have about your authenticity |

Figure 6.1. The Formula: $P = A + U - S$

P: Probability That High Performers Will Come to You

In a nutshell, the probability that high performers will find your organization appealing enough to exert the mental and physical effort required to apply for a job there is a function of the following three things:

1. **High performers have to feel an attraction to your unique culture (your Brown Shorts).** This means that they have to understand the two big dimensions of your Brown Shorts: number one is what differentiates your culture from all other organizations and number two is what separates high and low performers within your organization.

2. **High performers need to feel some urgency to leave their current situation.** If they're truly happy and fulfilled at their present job, they won't leave. So we need to help them understand and reflect on both the demotivators they now face and the motivators that are missing from their current situation.

3. **You can make all the pitches you want, but high performers are quite good at sniffing out subterfuge.** Any whiff of inauthenticity (for example, your pitch doesn't match your reality) is going to raise their suspicions and significantly detract from any attraction or urgency they may feel. This then lowers the probability that they'll apply for the job with you.

It's critical to fully grasp the P = A + U − S Brown Shorts Recruiting Formula, so I'm going to break it down and explain each piece of it. After I do that, I'll show you how the formula works in action. (We'll dissect an example of a typical job ad and then write a better one.) And finally, we'll talk about other recruiting situations, such as internal recruiters, networking, and social media.

A: Attraction High Performers Feel to Your Organization's Brown Shorts

Why would you leave a place where you're perfectly comfortable just to go someplace else that's indistinguishable from the place you are? Or, to put it another way, if you've just been seated at a restaurant you know you like, why would you immediately get up and drive across town to another restaurant that offers an identical dining experience? But what if you suddenly hear there's something different about that other place, something that intrigues you? In that case, you might make a hasty excuse to your server and run right over there to check it out.

It's a fascinating exercise to read your own job ads and ask "How many other companies could say the identical thing that we're saying?" In other words, how much incentive are you giving high performers to leave their comfortable environments and go somewhere else? While writing this chapter I needed a break, so I took an hour (or two) and started clicking around CareerBuilder.com to read some job ads. (When I party, I really party!) CareerBuilder.com is the largest online job site in the United States. It's very easy to search, so I had some fun. (Later I'll tell you about some cool recruiting research their company president, North America, recently gave me.)

I did a search for programmer jobs and selected a bunch from major companies. Then I started reading. And reading.

And reading. And then my eyes started glazing over. After a while, I couldn't tell any of these companies apart because each sounded exactly the same as the others. Some of the ads were written, some were delivered with slick videos, but holy mackerel, regardless of format, they all sounded the same.

To ensure I wasn't just imagining the similarities I clipped the key phrases used in the various ads so I could hold them up against each other and scrutinize their similarities. You know how most job ads begin with a paragraph about why we're wonderful (when we were founded, how many clients we have, how big we are, how many awards we've won)? Table 6.1 compares four of those big brand-name companies' terms, highlighting why they're different from everybody else. (Note: Company 1 and Company 2 are competitors, and Company 3 and Company 4 are competitors.)

Table 6.1.   Comparison of Key Phrases from Online Job Ads

Company 1	Company 2	Company 3	Company 4
Dedicated passionate coworkers	Potential passion	Help turn ideas into successful products	We are a leading global provider
Focus on exceptional customer service	Growth opportunities	Join a global leader	Join our team and make a difference
Tremendous opportunities for professional growth	Possibilities	Your next strategic career move is here	Our employees are the source of our strength

To be honest, it's possible I got mixed up and put some of those phrases under the wrong company. But can you blame me? Someone with a contentious nature *could* make the argument that there are subtle differences among them. But come on; let's be real—these companies are all pretty much saying the same thing. My memory's usually pretty sharp, and I devoted significant time to reading these job posts. And yet, I really couldn't tell you which company was which. The good news for job seekers is that fantastic opportunities abound, with all sorts of passionate coworkers, endless career opportunities, jobs that really make a difference, and all done on a global scale. (Once again, I hope my sarcasm is coming through.)

I'm fairly certain these companies distinguish their products and services better than they do their job openings. After all, they have billions of dollars in sales that would suggest a competent sales message. But if you're an employee at Company 1, with dedicated passionate coworkers, a focus on exceptional customer service, and tremendous opportunities for professional growth, where's the giant magnet in Company 2's potential, passion, growth, opportunities, and possibilities that's going to pull you away?

I have no idea what phrases like "dedicated passionate coworkers" or "tremendous opportunities for professional growth" really mean. For instance, what does a dedicated passionate coworker do that's different from what a coworker who's neither dedicated nor passionate does? Now, left to my own devices, I could make a list a mile long: dedicated passionate coworkers don't make excuses or point fingers when things go wrong, they work as long as necessary every day to complete the day's projects, they volunteer to take on new projects, and they generate at least 10 feasible ideas for improving efficiency every month. That's my list, and it may have nothing to do with Company 1's definition of dedicated passionate coworkers. But because they've given me no specifics on what these behaviors look like, I have only my own interpretations to rely on.

Remember what I said about Behavioral Specificity back when you were discovering your Brown Shorts, and how important it was to define specific behaviors and not fall victim to fuzzy language disease? And remember the quick three-part test I gave you to assess if you're getting enough Behavioral Specificity?

- Have you identified the specific behaviors?
- Could two strangers have observed those behaviors?
- Could two strangers have graded those behaviors?

If you're going to catch the interest of the high performers, your job ads have to include Behavioral Specificity, and they have to be able to pass this same three-part test. High performers want to know what differentiates your culture from all the other organizations out there. But those top candidates aren't going to get that with the indeterminate language found in most job ads.

In fact, I just searched the phrase "opportunities for professional growth" using double quotes ("/") so that my search engine would consider only the exact words in that exact order without any change. Even so, I still got 672,000 results. And without quotes, I get about 13 million results. I also did the same search on Bing and got 59 million results. No matter how you slice it, pitches like "dedicated passionate coworkers" or "tremendous opportunities for professional growth" are bland and generic. They aren't words that provide any real meaning, and they're not going to attract the right attention. Pitches like this are also one of the big reasons why only 10 percent of executives can say they are doing an excellent job at sourcing the right talent.

The most important lesson that came out of my little stroll through CareerBuilder is the need for Brown Shorts in your recruiting efforts. The first rationale driving the Brown Shorts concept is that these characteristics make your culture distinct from everybody else's. And that distinction is what you want to sell in your job ad, not some bland and generic description that makes you sound like everyplace else.

The second rationale driving the Brown Shorts concept is that these key cultural characteristics distinguish between your high and low performers. High performers are as unique as the organizations that call them high performers. So there aren't many universal truths we can say about high performers. But we can say with confidence that all high performers want to remain high performers, so you need to tell them all the great things that being a high performer in your organization means. And that includes all the low performer traits your organization simply doesn't tolerate. High performers don't like working with low performers, and they want to know that you don't like working with them either.

Think back for a moment to Chapter 3 on developing Brown Shorts Interview Questions. Table 6.2, a repeat of Table 3.1 shown here for your convenience, summarizes Company X's Brown Shorts.

Table 6.2.   Review of Company X's Brown Shorts

Positive Brown Shorts	Negative Brown Shorts
High performers are highly collabora- tive. They help each other out without being asked, and without any expecta- tion of recognition or reward.	Low performers routinely want indi- vidual recognition rather than share recognition with the larger team.
High performers share constructive thoughts and reactions without making their colleagues defensive, angry, or embarrassed.	Low performers share constructive ideas in ways that belittle, embarrass, or anger their colleagues.
High performers take personal respon- sibility for the quality and timeliness of their work without blame or excuses. If they do have problems, they solve them and then they share the problems and solutions with others so that everyone else can learn from their issues.	Low performers blame others—col- leagues and customers—when things go wrong, and say things like "I couldn't get it done because . . ." or "It's somebody else's fault."
High performers are self-directed learners. If they don't know how to do something, they actively find the neces- sary information or other resources to help them gain the skills and knowledge they need.	Low performers have a negative dis- position. When faced with a new situ- ation they regularly respond with the reasons why something will *not* work rather than try to figure out ways to achieve success.

Looking again at these two lists gives me a clear picture of what makes Company X different from every other company. I understand what it takes to be a high performer in its culture. From just this short list of Brown Shorts characteristics, I know that if I'm the kind of person who wants to work for a company that will hand me training, skills, and professional opportuni- ties on a silver platter, I'm not going to be happy at Company X. But if I'm a collaborative, self-directed learner with a penchant for problem solving who shows up to work every day with a positive attitude, I'm going to be interested. And my interest gets even stronger when I perceive that this culture doesn't tolerate the kind of low performers (those looking for the silver platter treatment) who annoy me and make my work experiences less pleasant. I certainly didn't get that insight when I read a job post boasting: "opportunities for professional growth."

Of course, there's a reason why so many companies use these generic, overused, and uninspiring phrases in their job ads. Self-destructive recruiting tendencies lead organizations to try to sound appealing to every job seeker on the planet. They think if they're bland and inoffensive enough everyone will want to work for them. You see this coming through in proud announcements such as "Today was a great day—we got 100 new applications in response to our ad." I've even witnessed celebrations taking place over record numbers of applications received. However, it doesn't matter how many people apply to a job posting; the only thing that matters is how many of the right people apply, make the initial cut, accept your offer, and turn into high performers. All companies track how many people apply, but how many track those other objectives?

Including your Brown Shorts in your recruitment efforts will attract the right candidates. Some people still argue that using Brown Shorts in recruiting is too exclusionary, and they don't want to chase away potential applicants. "If I'm not a self-directed learner," they'll say, "I'll be put off by that characteristic and I won't apply." To which I say, "Great!" You don't want people who are wrong for your culture to even apply in the first place. So the sooner those folks get cut out of the picture, the less work it means for you, and the more time it allows you to focus on potential high performers. So go ahead and use your Brown Shorts in your recruitment efforts because not only are your Brown Shorts going to attract the attention of the people you want, they're going to chase away the people you don't want.

Let's return to first part of the Brown Shorts Recruiting Formula, P = A + U − S. To increase the Probability of high performers applying to your company, your recruiting message must hold an element of Attraction. And the best way to do that is to use your Brown Shorts (who you are as a culture and what separates your high and low performers) as part of the main focus of your recruiting message.

U: Urgency High Performers Feel to Leave Their Current Situation

If a high performer is already working someplace that she considers truly outstanding, attraction alone isn't going to be enough to woo her away. You're going to have to provide an extra push that makes her rethink just how outstanding her current situation is. The good news here is that most companies don't do a great job at engaging and fulfilling their high performers. So you actually have a shot at influencing someone who thinks she's happy at her job to suddenly feel an urgency to go someplace better. You just need to help her understand her Shoves and Tugs.

Everybody has Shoves and Tugs, and it's a technique Leadership IQ commonly includes in our leadership training. Shoves are those issues that demotivate you, drain your energy, stop you from giving 100 percent, and make you want to quit (they "shove" you out the door). Tugs are those issues that motivate and fulfill you, make you want to give 100 percent, and keep you coming back every day (they "tug" at you to stay).

This concept seems simple enough. But here's the twist: Shoves and Tugs are *not* flip sides of the same coin. Just because somebody has lots of Tugs coming up this week does not mean he doesn't have any Shoves.

Let me begin with an "out there" analogy to help clarify this issue. Like Shoves and Tugs, Pain and Pleasure are also not opposites of each other. The opposite of pleasure isn't pain; it's just the absence of pleasure. Similarly, the opposite of pain isn't pleasure; it's just the absence of pain. If somebody is hitting my foot with a hammer, that's pain. And when they stop, that's not pleasure, it's just no more pain. If I'm getting the world's greatest back rub, that's pleasure. When it's gone, that's not pain, it's just no more pleasure.

Here's the lesson: if I'm getting a great back rub, it does not preclude somebody from hitting my foot with a hammer. And if that happens, the pain in my foot will totally detract from the pleasure I'm getting from the back rub. Here's a corollary lesson: If you walk past me one day and see someone hitting my foot with a hammer, you cannot fix the pain by giving me a back rub. In other words, you can't decrease the pain of my Shoves by trying to placate me with Tugs. The only way to stop the pain in my foot is to stop the hammer from hitting my foot. The only way to alleviate my work dissatisfaction is to take away my Shoves.

I told you this was a weird analogy, but here's why it's relevant. Every day, in organizations around the world, employees' feet are being hit with hammers, and their boss's solution isn't to stop the hammering (eliminate the Shove), but rather to give them a back rub (offer a Tug).

Consider, for example, a software development team in Silicon Valley led by a manager named Chris. The department was on heavy deadline to finish a new product, and more than a few of the organization's high performers were frustrated with the situation. Chris's recent anxiety had caused him to start micromanaging and instituting numerous useless meetings. He was also concerned because one of the low performers on the team had complained about the emotional intensity in the department, so he decided everyone would have to take a one-hour lunch together to decompress. The net effect of this situation was that the high performers were having to make up the work at home.

Instead of relieving stress, Chris's group-lunch mandate sparked even more unhappiness and grumbling. And as the grumbling grew, rather than ask his team about the source of their frustration (in other words, inquire about their Shoves), Chris decided to take the whole team to Catalina Island for the weekend to relax (he brought in a Tug). He figured it was a great way to offer a nice reward and get everyone's brain back into the game. When he made the announcement, you could almost see a few of the programmers' heads exploding. The last thing they wanted was more time with each other just hanging out and not working. They wanted to finish the project, to hit the deadline, and then go home and see their families. They wanted to stop wasting time at work and just get the job done.

Chris made the mistake of trying to fix a Shove with a Tug, and it couldn't have backfired more. Yes, Catalina Island is beautiful, and perhaps in another circumstance it would have been a nice reward. But his team was getting Shoved by too much time away from actual programming, and then came the boss with a Tug that actually involved even more time away from programming. Not only was the Tug a poor choice, but Chris's credibility was shot; he seemed obtuse and insensitive for not understanding what was really demoralizing his team.

A similar situation occurred in a hospital experiencing a major nursing shortage. Management implemented mandatory overtimes which made everyone tired and stressed. In an effort to make things better, management threw a big picnic for the nurses, something that, before the shortage, had made their nurses really happy.

But in the face of the obvious Shoves, the Tug didn't work. Attendance at the picnic was spotty, and those who did attend could be heard saying "Why couldn't they have taken the money they wasted on this picnic and hired a new nurse?" and "Do they really think they can buy us off like five year olds with a picnic? Do they really think we can't tell the difference?"

Both these examples show that when good employees encounter Shoves such as working with low performers, fighting through roadblocks, or enduring a terrible working environment, it's like getting hit on the foot with a hammer. And great Tugs like autonomy, having control over a process, and the opportunity to work on innovative projects aren't going to mean a thing until the Shove pain is taken away.

Clearly, this is an area where you've got some recruiting opportunity. Amazingly, a lot of the high performers who will tell you that they're happy in their current positions often feel Shoved and not very Tugged. Or, as we saw in the examples, they feel like the boss tries to minimize their Shoves by delivering Tugs instead of just making those Shoves go away. In other words, they could be happier—they just hadn't thought about it in those terms before. But if you can get them focused on the frustration they feel over their Shoves and Tugs, you're going to create a crack in their happiness, and they might think about finding someplace that offers a better ratio of Tugs to Shoves. Conveniently, since you're the one who got them thinking along these lines in the first place, you're also right there, front and center, saying "I feel your pain and I can make it go away." You just have to be able to speak to those Shoves and Tugs issues clearly, and it will resonate with any high performer currently feeling the imbalance of those issues.

Even CEOs have Shoves and Tugs. The Executive Director at ExecuNet shared some fascinating research with me. (Execu-Net is a membership organization dedicated to helping executives make smart career moves and better business decisions.) In a 2010 study of nearly 1,500 executives, ExecuNet found that 92 percent of CEOs and 94 percent of all other management respondents say leaders can be engaged in their work and with their employer but still open to considering new career opportunities with other organizations. Whether you're recruiting for the front lines or the executive suite, Shoves and Tugs will direct you to the right message.

Of course, this leads to two big questions: First, how do you discover the Shoves and Tugs of the people you'd like to recruit? And second, can you really work this information into a recruiting pitch like a job ad?

The first question is easily answered. If you want to know people's Shoves and Tugs, you just need to ask them. And the following two questions are typically all it takes:

1. Can you describe a time(s) in the past few months when you felt demotivated (or frustrated or emotionally burned out or whatever words sound like something you would say)?

2. Can you describe a time(s) in the past few months when you felt motivated (or excited or jazzed up, or however you might naturally express this)?

So, to whom do you ask these questions? Well, your recruiters can typically access this information fairly easily. If your recruiters are out chatting with folks, building relationships, and deepening your talent pipelines, they're already in direct communication with the kind of people whose answers to these questions will mean something to you. And not only can your recruiters ask these questions, but what they learn from the answers allows them to recruit more effectively. Of course, as you aggregate the answers to these questions, you'll know how your recruiting pitch needs to sound in order to elicit an emotional reaction from the folks who are living these Shoves and Tugs.

If you don't have recruiters, or even if you do, there's another pool of folks who can answer these Shoves and Tugs questions: your current high performers. Most of your high performers probably came from somewhere else. Ask them about the Shoves and Tugs they experienced before they joined you. Remember, your high performers all share the same Brown Shorts attitudes. They aren't clones of each other, but they do have many sensibilities in common, and Shoves and Tugs are some of them. Your high performer data pool is particularly interesting because these employees did ultimately join you, and that allows you to get both before and after pictures. Knowing what Shoves caused them to feel enough urgency to apply to your company tells you what kind of recruiting pitch you should be making to attract other high performers like them.

Parenthetically, in the course of asking your high performers these questions, you may discover that they are experiencing Shoves and Tugs at your company. You'll want to address that issue before a recruiter from another company uses this same technique on your people. To learn how to do that you can read my book *Hundred Percenters* or go to www.leadershipiq.com and check out our training modules under the eLearning tab.

After you get a group of data points, you'll see some patterns. You may discover that the high performers you want to recruit experience lots of Shoves about a lack of meaningful goals, or a lack of coaching and mentoring, or a lack of communication from senior executives. By the way, those aren't hypothetical Shoves; those are some of the big ones we discovered in our Global Talent Management Survey (see the full report at www.leadershipiq.com/hiring). Or you may learn that the high performers you want to recruit aren't getting enough Tugs about seeing the end result of their work, or assuming leadership roles, or learning new skills, or having more autonomy.

The Shoves and Tugs you'll hear are going to vary wildly from group to group. That notwithstanding, the following three Shoves are common among high performers.

Shove Number 1: Being a High Performer Stinks

Imagine it's Friday afternoon at 4 P.M., and the board requests a major report due on Monday at 9 A.M. This report could derail your career if it's not done right, and you're going to need help getting it done. You and someone else are in for a rough weekend of hard work, but a deadline is a deadline. So who are you going to turn to for help, the employee who gives 100 percent effort, or the employee who gives 50 percent effort? Obviously, you're going to turn to the high performer who gives 100 percent effort.

Now, say a similar situation happens again the next week. Who do you call on to make the painful sacrifice this time? Once again, it's the high performer. And what about the next time, and the next, and the next? You're always going to lean on your highest performing employees.

Now, answer this question: Who has the worst job in your company (and any company)? Say it with me—the high performer.

Shove Number 2: The Boss Can't Tell the Difference Between High Performers and Middle Performers

Imagine you've got two employees who just met a deadline for a very tough project. Leslie is a high performer who did an incredible job and gave 100 percent effort. Pat, on the other hand, is a middle performer who did a passable job. He didn't make any glaring mistakes, but he didn't do nearly as good a job as Leslie. Now they're both standing in front of you waiting for your feedback. Here's what the typical manager says: "Leslie and Pat, thanks for getting this done on time. Good work."

So what did Pat and Leslie just learn? Pat learned that giving 50 percent and doing passable work is totally fine. He's thinking, "Heck, giving 100 percent must be for chumps if we get the same feedback." And Leslie learned that giving 100 percent doesn't get noticed. She's thinking, "Why am I beating my brains out to give 100 percent when the boss seems to think 50 percent is just as good?"

Leadership IQ doesn't just teach hiring; we're also a leader in the world of employee engagement surveys. So we have data from hundreds of thousands of employees about just this issue, and we know that more than 70 percent of people consistently say that high performers should receive more rewards and recognition than others. But our data tell us that fewer than 20 percent of employees say that's what actually happens. This is a huge potential Shove, just sitting there waiting for you to take advantage of.

Shove Number 3: The Bloom Comes Off the Rose

While I'm discussing employee engagement, there's one more Shove you should know about. This year, Leadership IQ released a study about the link between employee engagement and employee tenure (like our other studies, you can read the whole report at www.leadershipiq.com/hiring). We analyzed more than 100,000 employees surveys, and we found that engagement scores generally drop steadily for the first 10 years of employees' tenure.

Please note, for background, our employee engagement survey uses a seven-point scale (I noted in Chapter 5 why you should use this instead of a five-point scale), so all these scores are out of a possible 7.

As can be seen in Figure 6.2, the typical employee is fairly engaged during Year 1 of work, with scores around 6.2 out of 7. But it's all downhill from there. By Year 4 the typical employee's scores have dropped to 5.4 (not the worst ever, but not great). Then the scores pop back up for Year 5 to a whopping 5.6. But

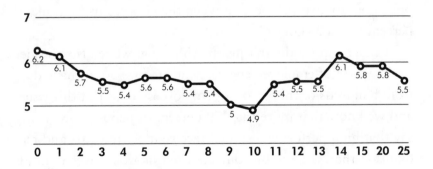

Figure 6.2. Employee Engagement

then they drop every year after that until they bottom out at 4.9 at Year 10. That's not a good score, and it represents a roughly 27 percent drop.

People talk about a seven-year itch, but the Leadership IQ data show it's really more like a ten-year disengagement. Assuming you have employees who have been with you longer than 10 years, the news gets better; scores start going back up. In fact, they go all the way back up to a 6.1 at Year 14. Unfortunately, they then start going back down again.

Additionally, when we crossmatched the tenure data to the age of those employees, we found that the 30 to 40 year olds with 6 to 10 years of tenure at a company had the lowest engagement scores. These folks just weren't motivated to give 100 percent effort, nor were they particularly inclined to recommend the company as a great organization to work for. The bloom had come off the rose.

Two big lessons come out of this. First, if you're not analyzing your employee engagement data like this, you should be, or you need to call somebody like Leadership IQ to do it for you. Because while it's great to recruit and hire high performers, it's not going to do you a whole lot of good if their engagement steadily drops year after year.

The second lesson is that while this could be seen as bad news, it could also be seen as a recruiting opportunity. Knowing that more of the bloom is coming off the rose every year for the first 10 years of an employee's tenure can help you narrow your recruiting pool. And it can help you identify people who might be sufficiently Shoved at their current employer so that they can be Tugged by you. Bear in mind that just because these folks are disengaged at one place does not mean they'll automatically be engaged for you, but it's still good data to have.

Shoves and Tugs in Job Ads

I still have to answer the other big question posed earlier: can you really work this Shoves and Tugs information into a recruiting pitch like a job ad? The short answer is yes, and here's how.

Imagine you're out on a date. Now, let's say you really want to win that date over, become the only person in the room he or she can see or hear. We're talking full-blown smitten here. How do you think you should start out—by talking about yourself or by talking about your date?

Almost everyone answers the question correctly. Of course, you talk about your date. But here's the shocker. In the recruiting world, another place you want to quickly capture the positive attention of another person, almost everybody gets it wrong. This destroys a lot of recruiting pitches. Let me prove it to you: More than 90 percent of job ads begin with a paragraph like this:

Jobs at the ACME Corporation

ACME Corp. is a top-tier solutions firm that provides information technology, systems engineering, and professional services to customers in the public and private sectors. With 30,000 professionals worldwide, the company has the customer knowledge, technical expertise, and proven performance to manage large-scale, mission-critical IT programs. With fiscal year 2010 sales of $XX billion, ACME Corp. is the third-largest company in our industry. Our vision is to be our customers' first choice in each and every market we serve. To earn our customers' trust and meet their individual needs, we will provide valued solutions with the best prices, products, and services that make our customers' lives easier. But we're not finished. We're on our way to even bigger and better things. Providing superior customer service requires superior people.

Unless you're attending a narcissist's convention, this opening is terrible. You don't even have to read every line to feel the automatic turnoff. This ad is all about "us": when we were founded, how many clients we have, how big we are, how many awards we've won. In the blind-date equivalent of this ad, you'd be sitting alone at the bar before the first round of drinks arrived. It doesn't matter if you're recruiting one person or a thousand; the only way to grab high performers' attention is to open your pitch by discussing the issues that matter to them, and whether or not you can meet their needs.

Neurologically speaking, the opening paragraphs of your ad (the first few minutes you have someone's attention) are the most important. Your candidates form their opinions about you during those first precious moments. Then their brains decide whether or not to allocate any more neurological energy to listening to what you have to say.

Let's jump back to the dating scene for a minute. Perhaps you've heard of a free online dating site called OkCupid. Now, I married my high school sweetheart, so I'm not there trolling for dates. However, as a researcher, I am impressed with their statistics. OkCupid has an advanced statistics shop, called OkTrends, where they study the hundreds of millions of OkCupid user interactions. In one study they looked at the kinds of words men use in their opening messages to women in order to learn what does (and doesn't) generate a reply. If you're not familiar with how online dating works, basically, you check out people's profiles on the website, and if you like what you read, you send that person a message and hope you get a response. (And then, maybe after that, you meet for an actual date, like we used to do in the olden days.)

You can just imagine the cheesy messages that the study revealed don't work, meaning that women did not reply to the man's message. But "you mention," "noticed that," and "curious what" all generated positive responses. (Statistically, messages with those phrases received double the normal response rates.)

If a man appears to have read a woman's profile, and shows knowledge and interest in the things she's interested in, he's got a much greater chance of hearing back from her. A good message would sound like this: "**You mention** that you like cooking and **I noticed that** you travelled to Italy. **I am curious what** your favorite region was in terms of cuisine." That's the kind of guy we fathers might let our daughters date. (I also have a son, and when he hits dating age, he will be forced to read all this research.)

Whether you're dating to find the perfect match or recruiting to find the perfect match, always start your interactions by talking about the other person and his or her interests. Let people know that you know what they want to hear about, that you are sensitive to what they want to gain from this interaction, and that you care about the same things that they care about. And again, if you don't know what their interests are (their Shoves and Tugs), you need to do some research and figure it out.

Potential candidates are interested in learning how you can offer the Tugs they want and eliminate the Shoves they're suffering. This sounds like heresy, I know, but they really don't care how long you've been in business or how many awards you've won. At this point let's look back at the terrible example paragraph from ACME Corp. shown on Page 168.

Is somebody not going to apply because you don't have enough employees or awards? Are they really sitting there thinking, "Well, I would have applied, but they only have 30,000 employees and $10 billion in sales and I have a strict rule that I will only work for companies with over 40,000 employees and over $15 billion in sales"?

People care about whatever they care about, and that's what you need to give them. Meet their needs, and you'll attract them. Don't and you won't. In a little bit you'll see an example of a Brown Shorts recruitment pitch—a much better way for you to start.

S: Suspicions They Have About Your Authenticity

The final piece of the Brown Shorts Recruiting Formula is the extent to which the people you're trying to recruit harbor suspicions that your claims may not be true. Sure, they may think your culture sounds great, and you seem to understand their Shoves and Tugs. But does this all sound authentic? Is this what it's really like to work inside your organization? Or is it just a smoke screen you're blowing to make it sound like an attractive place to work?

Authenticity is a simple concept—just show who you really are. This is easier said than done, of course, but it's an important concept nonetheless. The good news is that if you stay focused on engaging people with Brown Shorts and Shoves and Tugs, you'll eliminate any suspicions about your authenticity.

Suspicions mostly arise when we use language that isn't specific enough. (Go back to everything I've said so far about the need for Behavioral Specificity.) It's easy enough to see this in the bad example job ad we've been using on Page 168. Look it over again at this point.

Does that ad sound like it was written by, or even reflects the feelings of, real employees? Or does it sound like corporate MBA gobbledygook that means nothing even though it went through about 20 committees, 10 lawyers, and a week of offsite developmental meetings? I'm going to vote for the gobbledygook. Ad copy like this always begs the question "Why can't the real people tell us what they actually think?"

Authenticity isn't just a huge issue for job ads, it's also critical if you intend to recruit with social media. I mentioned earlier that I spent some time with Brent Rasmussen, President of North America for CareerBuilder. Brent shared some fascinating data from a few of the recent studies. Based on a 2010 CareerBuilder survey of 2,800 workers who use social media, the top issues job seekers want to see on company social media pages are:

- Job listings—35 percent
- Fact sheet on the company—26 percent
- Career paths within the organization—23 percent
- Something that conveys fun about working for the organization—16 percent
- Employee testimonials—16 percent

And from that same survey, the top turnoffs are:

- Communications read like an ad—38 percent
- Failure to respond to questions—30 percent
- Failure to regularly post information or blog entries—22 percent
- Removed/filtered comments—22 percent
- Inconsistency in messaging in different social media sites—19 percent

The lesson: Be real, be authentic, share your Brown Shorts, and don't worry about appearing attractive to the people who don't want to wear your Brown Shorts (they're not a good fit for you anyway). Don't try to be something you're not in your recruitment efforts, or you'll fail to attract all the high performers who would fit your culture.

And don't think those high performers won't find out if you're not being real. One of CareerBuilder's hot new applications is called Work@, which enables employees to share open jobs at their company with personal and professional contacts within their Facebook network. It's a pretty open and transparent world right now, and it doesn't look as if that's going to change anytime soon. So remember—be authentic, and you'll be OK.

PUTTING THE FORMULA TO WORK

Here again is the P = A + U − S formula broken down into its component parts. Review it and then let's return to our bad job ad example on Page 168. Let's see if we can fix it using what we've just learned.

P		A		U		S
Probability of high performers applying to your company	=	Attraction they feel to your organization's Brown Shorts	+	Urgency they feel to leave their current situation	–	Suspicions they have about your authenticity

Clearly there aren't any Brown Shorts described in the ad that could Attract potential candidates. There's also nothing that increases the Urgency (Shoves and Tugs) someone might feel to leave his or her current situation. And this ad actually increases my Suspicion because it is in no way linked to employees' everyday reality. So our formula tells us that there's a frighteningly low Probability that a currently employed high performer will exert much (if any) effort to apply for a job with us.

So how do we fix this ad? Earlier I said that an opening paragraph should talk about the candidate and not present a list of boring and narcissistic corporate mumbo jumbo. Let's pretend you did a little digging with your recruiters and your current high performers, and you discovered some Shoves and Tugs your potential recruits are probably experiencing. You learned that in their current jobs they're feeling Shoves in time wasted by people playing politics with blame and finger-pointing. They're also being Shoved because they're working with low performers who spend more time picking apart ideas than developing solutions. And they're not getting the Tugs from working collaboratively on teams that brainstorm and implement solutions because of the politicized and territorial workplaces they're currently in.

Let's further pretend that you've discovered the Brown Shorts in your own company and you know that high performers are:

- Highly collaborative. They help each other out without being asked and without any expectation of recognition or reward.
- Empathic toward customers' and colleagues' needs They don't get angry or blame, they sincerely and earnestly try to understand and help.

You also know that low performers:

- Want individual recognition. They don't want to share recognition with the larger team.
- Blame others—colleagues and customers—when things go wrong. They give excuses such as "I couldn't get it done because . . ." or "It's somebody else's fault."

In addition to all that insight, let's assume this job ad is for a programmer and that an absolute requirement is a B.S. in computer science (this was required for the real-life ad). So let's rewrite that first paragraph using our Brown Shorts in the following way.

Join the ACME Team!

Wouldn't you rather be writing code than playing corporate politics? Did you get a degree in computer science so you could design amazing software or did you do all that hard work so you could waste time finger-pointing in a mind-numbing meeting? At ACME Corp. our thousands of computer scientists and engineers work together and share credit. In fact, glory hogs don't last very long here. Nor do people who tear down others' ideas instead of developing their own. When smart people collaborate instead of compete, amazing things happen. If you haven't had the chance yet, check out our XYZ Software that runs 87 percent faster than anything else on the market. We also collaborate with our customers. We bend over backwards (and maybe do some flips) to make sure they're happy. We don't screen their calls—we love hearing from them.

We'll be honest; ACME Corp. isn't for everybody. If you hate collaborating and sharing credit, or if spending hours with customers annoys you, then we're probably not for you. But if you've got a big brain and you'd like to use it for making cutting-edge software (and not for making excuses), then you need to apply. Now.

To be sure, this pitch isn't for everybody. If a pitch like this doesn't match your Brown Shorts, if it doesn't reflect the Shoves and Tugs that your candidates are experiencing, then, it's useless. But for the imaginary ACME Corp., it would work very well.

As I noted earlier, don't get hung up on this being a job ad. This isn't about job ads; it's about recruiting pitches. Bland corporate speak gobbledygook doesn't work when delivered by a recruiter, in a video, at a career fair or networking event, or posted on LinkedIn and Facebook. In fact, a bad pitch will get your company killed in the social media world.

According to our Global Talent Management Survey, employee referrals are the best source for hiring high performers. The best. I had two reactions when I saw the statistics. First, employee referrals work so well because they fulfill the formula ($P = A + U - S$) better than anything else. By definition referrals are authentic—how could they not be, since they come from actual employees. My second thought was that if we put the culturally specific and authentic messaging into our job ads and recruiting, we could improve their effectiveness as well.

By the way, there are some other people who are making the same points that I'm making here. In a 2011 study of 5,600 workers nationwide, CareerBuilder asked about factors that made people less likely to apply for jobs. The first three factors were failure to include salary range, unclear or nondescriptive job titles, and failure to include company name. The fourth issue, which is relevant to our discussion here, was a dull job description.

You don't have to (nor should you) take my word for any of this; you should test it for yourself. At Leadership IQ we test these types of pitches for our clients all the time. We discover their Brown Shorts, build their Brown Shorts Interview Questions, create their Answer Guidelines, and then we revamp their recruiting strategies, tactics, and messaging. We test every step. Parenthetically, while job ads may not be the only channel you use, they're the best one for testing your message quickly, quantitatively, and inexpensively.

In another example very similar to the previous one, we used the organization's original job ad as a control and then conducted a split test with a rewritten Brown Shorts ad to see which performed better. For background, a split test is a simple experimental design whereby you run two versions of a job ad (or marketing brochure, landing page, or whatever), altering certain aspects in each to see which performs better and why.

The trick with split testing is ensuring that the samples are perfectly split without any sampling errors or contamination. Once you get through split testing, you then move on to multivariate testing—testing multiple variables simultaneously—but that would take a statistics chapter alone to explain thoroughly. So we'll stick to split testing for the moment.

We ran this split test with the original (or generic) ad versus the Brown Shorts ad, and these are the results (rounded numbers):

Job Ad	Generic	Brown Shorts
Views	10,000	12,000
Applications	800	500
First Round	20	60
Finalist	3	18
Offer	1	8
Accepted	1	6

Let's summarize the results. The Brown Shorts ad received more views, meaning more people clicked on the ad and ostensibly looked at it, or at least quickly skimmed it (12,000 vs. 10,000). But the Brown Shorts ad had fewer people apply for the job (500 vs. 800). Clearly, when you write a job ad with some exclusionary language (like "we're not right for everybody"), you will exclude some people. But as I've said, your goal isn't the grand total of applicants, it's getting applications from high performers who will be a great fit in your organization.

Now, while the Brown Shorts ad had fewer responses than the generic ad, the applicants it did attract were of much higher quality. In fact, with the Brown Shorts ad, three times as many people made it through the first round of the hiring process (20 vs. 60). Sure, the generic ad got more people to apply, but they weren't the right people. The HR/recruiting team had to do a lot more work sorting through all those applicants with a lot less payoff. Additionally, the Brown Shorts ad had six times as many people get to the finalist stage (3 vs. 18), which led to eight times as many job offers (1 vs. 8) and six times as many accepted offers (1 vs. 6).

METRICS FOR HIRING

It's your choice as to how you measure success, but I tend to like results-oriented measures. I want to get high performers hired, not just reading my ads. Of course, helping our clients doesn't stop here; our measures keep right on going throughout the employee life cycle. Some of the metrics that we've found particularly useful include the following:

- **Quality of hire:** How effective are your new hires? You can measure this easily enough with your performance management system or even a survey. We usually recommend assessing at 3-, 6-, and 12-month intervals because this not only gives you on-the-job performance, but it also tells you how quickly these folks got up to speed. Note, though, that your performance management tool must include measures of attitude, not just technical skills.

- **New hire engagement:** With today's sophisticated employee engagement surveys (and yes, I mean the kind that Leadership IQ provides) it's simple to determine the engagement levels of your new hires. And since our definition of engagement includes the extent to which an employee is motivated to give 100 percent effort, engagement absolutely drives bottom-line results.
- **New hire tenure:** It's great to get new hires, and it's terrific for them to be productive and engaged, but it's even better when they also stay with you for a while.
- **Manager satisfaction:** How happy are your managers both with their new hires and the process used to get those new hires? The most common way of getting this data is with a short survey of your managers.

It's important to break down all of these measures by each recruiting channel. For example, you'll need to know how quality of hire compares for employees found through job ads vs. through recruiters vs. through career fairs vs. through employee referrals. This is how you'll make the smart decisions about where to focus your time and money.

RECRUITING CHANNELS

What recruiting channels are available to you? Well, there are quite a few, and some are more effective than others. In our Global Talent Management Survey we asked more than 1,000 companies which recruiting channels they found most effective for delivering high performing frontline employees. Here they are, starting with the channel deemed most effective at delivering high performers, and then working down from there.

1. Employee referrals
2. Networking
3. Online job boards
4. Company career portal
5. Company recruiters
6. Outside recruiters
7. Social networking sites
8. Career fairs
9. Job ads in print media
10. Research services

We also asked which of these channels did the best job at delivering high performing executives. You'll see the rankings changed quite a bit.

1. Networking
2. Outside recruiters
3. Employee referrals
4. Company recruiters
5. Company career portal
6. Online job boards
7. Social networking sites
8. Research services
9. Job ads in print media
10. Career fairs

These lists are always interesting, but they're even more interesting when you cut the data more deeply. For example, for companies that have thoroughly defined what differentiates their culture (Brown Shorts), these five channels were rated significantly more effective for recruiting frontline high performers:

1. Employee referrals
2. Networking
3. Online job boards
4. Company career portal
5. Company recruiters

For companies that have better financial performance than the companies in their industry, these four channels were rated significantly more effective for recruiting frontline high performers:

1. Employee referrals
2. Networking
3. Online job boards
4. Company career portal

And these same four channels were also significantly more effective for cultures with highly engaged employees.

The most important point I'd like everyone to take away from this is the extent to which defining and using your Brown Shorts can make all recruiting techniques significantly more effective. Throughout this chapter I've been showing you how your recruiting efforts, including job ads, can be made exponentially more effective. And I'm not the only one delivering this message.

Let's return to CareerBuilder's research. In their Applicant Experience survey of more than one million workers, Career-

Builder asked respondents about their perceptions of their interactions with representatives from various employers when applying for jobs. While 35 percent had a better perception of the employer after speaking with a company representative, 20 percent had a worse opinion. One in five workers (21 percent) didn't think the company representative was enthusiastic about the company being an employer of choice.

Soak that in for a minute. Not only aren't we fully selling ourselves, but we might actually be turning off potential candidates. The risk isn't just that we're not doing enough to effectively recruit, it's that we could be doing actual damage to our brand.

WEAR YOUR BROWN SHORTS EVERYWHERE

To sum this up, when you do everything I recommend, you get to wear your most comfortable clothes—your Brown Shorts— every day. Effective recruiting isn't about manufacturing a message; it's about revealing who you really are. Sure, you want to do that in a clever and compelling way, but it's better that your message be less produced and more authentic than the reverse.

I've probably watched more than a thousand corporate recruiting videos. Overwhelmingly, they're overproduced manufactured fluff pieces that don't give any sense for why this company is different from any other company. Nor do they explain why a high performer might want to join that company. Even worse, these videos are rarely tested for effectiveness. For example, do you know how many additional new hires came because you had a video? What were the performance evaluations of those new hires like a year later?

When you wear your Brown Shorts, whether it's in videos, ads, or a recruiter's spiel, you don't have to manufacture anything. You are who you are. (How's that for a tautology?) You already have high performers who fit your culture, and you want more people just like them. But the only way those high performers will want to join is if they can see the real you. Brown Shorts may not seem like haute couture, but they're all you—and that's what counts.

Here's one final statistic from our talent management study. Companies rated as having thoroughly defined what differentiated their Brown Shorts (culture) were able to hire their first-choice candidates 24 percent more often than companies that hadn't defined their Brown Shorts. The lesson here? The more clearly you define who you really are, the more you get the people you really want.

For free downloadable resources including the latest research, discussion guides, and forms please visit www.leadershipiq.com/hiring.

7

Put Your Brown Shorts to Work for More than Just Hiring

You now know how to effectively recruit the candidates you want. Together, your Brown Shorts, your Interview Questions, and your Answer Guidelines give you the tools you need to make a sophisticated apples-to-apples comparison of those candidates. You're now able to confidently select the candidates who are the best attitudinal fit for your organization. It's a lot to take in. But once it all has sunk in, new revelations will emerge about what else your Brown Shorts can do for you.

Here's one revelation that I like to see our clients, webinar attendees, certification trainees, and now our readers have. I'll break it down into a step-by-step process so you can see how the light bulb usually comes on.

1. The good and bad answers from the Brown Shorts
   Answer Guidelines came from actual employees of this
   organization.
2. Our own employees—people we have ostensibly
   trained—actually did (and probably still do) things that
   are in the bad column.
3. Thus the things we executives consider unacceptable is
   currently thought to be acceptable by a group of our
   employees.
4. That *either* means that we have employees who don't
   have the right attitude (we didn't do a good enough job
   selecting them) . . .
5. . . . *or* we haven't done a good enough job teaching
   these employees what's unacceptable here (we didn't
   explain why we consider the things in the bad answer
   column to be unacceptable).

So far this book has been focused on fixing Point 4: doing
a better job of hiring people with the right attitude. But here's
something very important: all the Brown Shorts work you do
to fix Point 4 will also help you fix Point 5. You will be able
to better instruct your current employees so they understand
exactly what differentiates high and low performance. This, in
turn, will result in a lot more of the high performance effort you
want.

When you did your Brown Shorts Discovery, you probably
learned that not everyone on your executive team shares the
exact same understanding about what defines high and low
performance. You corrected that by creating and sharing your
Brown Shorts. This then leads to the obvious conclusion that
your employees, the people under the leadership of those same

executives, probably also differ in their understanding of high and low performance.

And if that thought isn't enough to convince you to keep teaching employees your performance expectations, I can do even better. One of the benefits of Leadership IQ's prominence in the world of employee engagement surveys is that I have the data to prove the value of teaching performance expectations. Our surveys often ask employees to rate the statement "I understand whether my performance is where it should be." Frighteningly, only about 24 percent of employees feel like they really understand if their performance is where it should be. Another 28 percent are getting there (but don't feel like they truly understand), and 48 percent really don't know.

Those are not good numbers (and again, they're real numbers from real employees). It's a bad situation, analogous to a college student who, despite it being midsemester, has no idea if he's heading toward an A or an F. And while providing transparent performance feedback is not the only function that managers (and professors) have to fulfill, shouldn't it at least be one of the top five responsibilities?

WHY DON'T EMPLOYEES ALREADY KNOW THIS STUFF?

Employees don't know enough about the differences between high and low performance for two reasons. First, some companies don't believe they should have to teach it. And second, some companies aren't doing a good enough job effecting knowledge transfer—their teaching isn't getting through.

Regarding the first issue, I've had executives look me right in the eye and say, "I shouldn't have to spoon-feed people about the difference between high and low performance; they should just know it." When I hear that I think, "If you're truly doing a perfect job of hiring people with great attitudes who already understand everything you want, and can deliver it, then I suppose you can skip the detailed teaching." And that's true. If 100 percent of your employees are demonstrably high performers and you have 0 percent preventable errors (no defects service breakdowns, or missed handoffs), then you can confidently skip the whole teaching/coaching concept as well as this chapter. But how many of us can truly say that? And, ironically, the companies who could be excluded are only that self-assured because they already do such a good job of teaching high and low performance.

On the second issue, lots of companies just aren't teaching performance expectations well enough. I'm reminded of a behind-the-scenes football show about an NFL team during training camp. There was a scene with the third-string quarterback (who you just knew was going to get cut) asking the coach, "What can I do to get better?" To which the coach replied, "Just keep doing what you're doing."

The quarterback was pretty frustrated with the coach's answer. He didn't articulate his frustration well, so here's a distillation of what he said: "What I'm currently doing has gotten me to be a third-string quarterback! What should I do differently so that I can become second-string or even first-string?"

I recount this story because I see this same kind of scenario over and over again when I'm working with managers. "Keep doing what you're doing," they tell their people. To which any employee can justifiably respond, "Well, what I'm doing just got me put on a 90-day improvement plan, so do you have anything a little more specific?"

And once again, we find ourselves going back to Chapter 1 on finding your Brown Shorts and the need for Behavioral Specificity. I gave some examples of the euphemisms, admonitions, and clichés that pass for performance expectations these days.

High performing employees will . . .

- Maintain the highest standards of professionalism
- Treat customers as a priority
- Regard responsibility to the patient as paramount
- Demonstrate positive attitude and behavior
- Lead by example
- Engage in open, honest, and direct conversation
- Respect and trust the talents and intentions of their fellow employees
- Challenge the company's thinking

This kind of fuzzy language populates our Performance Appraisals, Codes of Conduct, Mission Statements, and more. But it doesn't really count as teaching or setting clear expectations.

Let's do a little comparison. Imagine that you're trying to get your employees to be more accountable, so you decide to set better performance expectations. Following are two different ways to do this. Both examples are excerpted from two different companies' performance appraisals, although both versions were also used in myriad other training and employee orientation formats. After all, if you're going to hold employees accountable for certain behaviors, it only makes sense that you would use those same behaviors to constantly and continuously teach employees about your expectations.

After you read both versions, I think you'll be able to see which company does a better job of setting expectations—and thus teaching employees—about accountability.

Version 1: This performance appraisal uses fairly common language, in standard paragraph format, for explaining accountability. For purposes of its performance appraisal, this company provided paragraphs, like the following one, on a variety of topics. It then asked managers to rate employees (on a scale of 1 to 5) on the extent to which the employees exemplified these behaviors. It's all standard stuff that you find being done in any number of organizations.

As an employee, I am considered accountable when I take responsibility for my own actions and decisions. I keep to my commitments, and when that's not possible, I notify the appropriate person and develop a Plan B. I act as a role model for accepting responsibility and being accountable, and I encourage others to do the same.

Version 2: Instead of Version 1's traditional paragraph, this example, shown in Table 7.1, explains accountability in three ways. The left column (Needs Work) describes the behaviors associated with someone who is not being accountable. The middle column (Good Work) describes an acceptable level of accountability, and the right column (Great Work) details the behaviors associated with a high level of accountability. (Note: I condensed the original descriptions in all three columns to provide a more succinct example.) For purposes of their performance appraisal, managers simply identified which employees belonged in which categories.

Now let's compare Version 1 and Version 2. Which of the two will likely do a better job of teaching employees what we

Table 7.1. Three Levels of Accountability (Word Picture)

Needs Work on Accountability	Good Work on Accountability	Great Work on Accountability
When new changes are implemented, I resist the changes and push for a return to the "status quo." When breakdowns or missed communications occur, I engage in finger-pointing and blaming others. When I make mistakes or miss deadlines, I offer excuses like "I couldn't get it done because. . . ." When the going gets tough or intense, I become frantic and even overreact. I avoid extra work, and when working in a team I allow my coworkers to do most of the work.	I openly support change initiatives. I don't wait to be told to take action, and I find opportunities to help complete projects more quickly and effectively. I accept personal responsibility for quality and timeliness of work without making excuses or blaming others. I meet my commitments, and if it looks like I won't personally be able to meet a commitment, I take responsibility for implementing an alternative that ensures the commitment still gets met.	I do everything in the Good Work category, plus . . . I encourage and convince my fellow employees to support change initiatives. I actively redirect conversations with my colleagues to stop them from making excuses or blaming others. If I uncover an unexpected problem, I immediately remedy the situation, but then I also bring it to the attention of others so that we can develop a root-cause solution and nobody else has to suffer through the same issue.

mean when we say "be accountable"? Feel free to give your own answer, but I've never actually had someone tell me that Version 1 was better. I've used this example, and asked this same question, in hundreds of speaking engagements, and the answer is always unanimous: Version 2 is the more effective teaching tool.

Version 2 is more effective by design—it was created specifically to be a great teaching tool. We call the technique behind

this example Word Pictures, and while we use it in many facets
of our training, it's a highly effective way to turn your Brown
Shorts into a tool for teaching performance expectations. When
used correctly, the Word Pictures technique clears up any performance misconceptions and shows your current employees
how they can exhibit the same high performer behaviors you're
looking for in your job candidates.

Word Pictures and Brown Shorts are like siblings. In fact,
once we help our clients develop their Brown Shorts, it's a
fairly straightforward process to immediately turn the Brown
Shorts into Word Pictures. With Word Pictures our clients have
a great teaching tool for use in orientations, onboarding, tenured employee training, performance appraisals, and coaching
discussions.

Word Pictures have many uses, and because you're already
so close to having them, it's important to take the time to
develop this leadership tool. After all, the goal of hiring high
performers is to get you more high performers (am I full of
insight, or what?). And all the work you're doing to hire more
high performers from outside of your company can now be used
to develop more high performers from within your company—
truly a win-win situation. For you fans of Charlie Sheen's glori-
ous month of nonstop chatter, we could call this "bi-winning."
You're winning here, and you're winning there.

WHY ARE WORD PICTURES SO POWERFUL?

Word Pictures have two important characteristics that drive
their effectiveness. And no, one of them is not because they are

longer than the generic paragraph in Version 1; I could write an entire page filled with nonsense, but it's not going to accomplish anything.

Behavioral Specificity

Word Pictures are powerful because, first, they require Behavioral Specificity. Word Pictures are exactly what the name tells you they are. You're going to paint a vivid and specific picture with your words. Your employees, upon hearing these vivid words, will be able to envision themselves exhibiting the behaviors the words describe. To that end, Word Pictures use the same three tests of Behavioral Specificity that I provided in Chapter 1.

- Could you identify the specific behaviors in each category?
- Could two strangers observe those behaviors?
- Could two strangers grade those behaviors?

And just to give you a heads-up, the toughest part about creating Word Pictures is making them specific enough to pass the observable and gradable tests. But they must pass these tests or they won't work in the real world. The good news is that your Brown Shorts Answer Guidelines can be distilled into a set of behaviorally specific lessons that can be generalized to all your employees. Or, to state it more simply, you can turn your Answer Guidelines into Word Pictures. So instead of teaching the differences between bad (Warning Signs) and good (Positive Signals) interview responses, you're now using those guidelines to teach the differences between bad and good performance (Needs Work, Good Work, and Great Work).

And that categorical distinction (Needs Work, Good Work, and Great Work) raises the second powerful aspect of Word Pictures: they're based on a scientifically robust learning theory called Concept Attainment.

Concept Attainment

In a nutshell, Concept Attainment involves learning through studying positive and negative examples. Do you remember the Sesame Street song "One of These Things Is Not Like the Other"? Well, that actually uses some advanced cognitive psychology—Concept Attainment. For example, to teach about the characteristics of a square, Grover or Big Bird has you look at a bunch of squares (the positive examples). But there's one triangle (the negative example) hanging out in the middle of all those squares. Or you learn about the characteristics of an apple by looking at lots of apples (positive examples) and then an orange (negative example) or a banana (negative example) or a pear (negative example). By analyzing those positive and negative examples, you quickly figure out the characteristics that define squares and apples.

Research tells us that you learn the characteristics of apples faster and more thoroughly with Concept Attainment than you do if you listen to a lecture on the characteristics of apples and then go out into the world and try to apply that abstract knowledge to specific situations. This same idea of Concept Attainment can be applied to performance-related learning. While a great deal of research shows people can learn by being told how to do something (positive examples), those same studies also show that people learn even more when they're also told how not to do something (negative examples). Or, as the poet William Blake said roughly 200 years ago "You never know what is enough unless you know what is more than enough."

Some of the greatest lessons you learned as a kid (and that you probably teach to your kids) are negative examples. Here are a few negative examples I've uttered to my kids in the past few days:

- Don't touch the hot stove.
- Don't put that thing in your mouth.
- Don't hit your brother/sister.
- Don't pick your nose.
- Don't stand in the hallway without clothes on.
- Don't talk with your mouth full.
- Don't take such a big bite.
- Don't touch the clean laundry with those grimy hands.
- Don't jump on the clean laundry.
- Don't stand on the furniture.
- Don't stage dive off my new chair.

I do also offer positive examples, but if you've ever taught by negative example, you know how effective it is. Using the cognitive psychology of Concept Attainment, we've discovered that employees learn a lot faster and more completely when they understand both what you want and what you don't want. Great teaching is not an either/or thing; it requires both positive and negative examples. Word Pictures are designed to provide both.

Since you already know about textual analysis from Chapter 5, I'll make one more comment here. Did you notice how the Word Pictures example in Version 2 used first person pronouns ("I do" instead of "you do" or "she does")? It's not a deal breaker, but using first person pronouns helps the people hearing your Word Pictures paint a better mental picture. They can more clearly imagine themselves engaged in those specific behaviors. Thus, each of the categories is kept behaviorally specific and distinct.

By the way, most of us learned about concepts like first person pronouns with Concept Attainment—positive and negative examples. You learned the definition of a first person pronoun by seeing positive examples ("I" or "me") and negative examples ("you, she, he," or "they"). We learn many things through Concept Attainment. In fact, if you pay attention to the positive and negative examples that you see in the next few days, I guarantee you'll be amazed by how many things you learn through Concept Attainment. Whether we plan for it or not, this kind of learning happens all the time. And once you realize what a great tool it is, you'll do that "I could've had a V8" head slap and wonder why you haven't used Word Pictures for employee training before.

WORD PICTURES WORK FOR ANY TOPIC

Word Pictures are a tool for teaching new and tenured employees. They're also a tool for onboarding and evaluating performance. Use Word Pictures when giving instructions or constructive feedback. And you can apply Word Pictures as the foundation of your performance appraisals or for identifying stellar performance so you can reward high performers. Word Pictures, instead of a bland Mission Statement, can be hung on your boardroom wall or in your lobby. Quite simply, Word Pictures are a scientifically advanced method for teaching employees.

To that end, you can teach employees virtually any performance topic using Word Pictures. Some of the performance-related Word Pictures we've created for our clients include: accountability, customer service, leadership, service excellence, ownership, responsibility, problem solving, creativity, collaboration, teamwork, open-mindedness, communication, innovation, leading by example, professionalism, confidence, leading change, discipline, initiation, emotional intelligence, patience, perseverance, purpose, trust, respect, shared values, meeting challenges head-on, exceeding expectations, efficiency, passion, fun, individual growth, analytical thinking, persistence, organization, commitment, courage, openness, dependability, focus, motivation, transparency, expertise, compromise, delegation, competition, accommodation, reward, abstract thinking, outcome focus, credibility, truth seeking, diversity, flexibility, tenacity, entitlement, achievement, critical feedback, proactive, problem solving, and more.

The topics you choose to present to your employees in Word Pictures are entirely up to you. But one of the keys to effective teaching is maintaining the interest of the people you're teaching. People learn best when they are inspired, challenged, and stimulated. And while Word Pictures certainly do all that, don't inundate your people with too many Word Pictures. Using Word Pictures to teach everything under the sun causes employees to grow apathetic and stop learning entirely. So choose your topics carefully.

Back in Chapter 1 I mentioned LifeGift, a not-for-profit organization that recovers organs and tissue for individuals needing transplants. As you can imagine, a lot of difficult and highly sensitive work transpires daily at LifeGift. Its mission is to get donors, which requires a lot of teamwork. But just like any organization, day-to-day activities at LifeGift can lead employees astray of that mission. To combat this, LifeGift approached its first foray into Word Pictures with the goal of teaching its people about working together. Specific issues of concern included engaging with management in other departments and staying focused on the company mission.

LifeGift invested some serious time into shaping its Word Picture. And when the shaping was done, it had a teaching tool that painted a picture of the desired behavioral characteristics that everyone in the organization could benefit from. Once completed, LifeGift introduced its Word Picture at the close of a weekly management meeting during a time traditionally reserved for discussing topics or issues relating to leadership.

As President and CEO Sam Holtzman attests, this Word Picture has allowed LifeGift's leaders to think along the same lines and to spread that message of performance expectation to every person in the organization. Since that time, individual departments have also been encouraged to develop Word Pictures, but Sam cautions them to choose their topics wisely. The characteristics the Word Picture describes must be broad and job related and not personal or subjective to a certain manager's interpretation of what's important.

Here's another Word Picture, this time highlighting leadership. Your organization may not define leadership this way, but Table 7.2 shows how Caesars Entertainment Corporation saw the issue.

Table 7.2.   Word Picture for Leadership

Needs Work on Leadership	Good Work on Leadership	Great Work on Leadership
I lead from behind my desk, giving directives mostly through memos or e-mails.	I gain support by building cooperation through personal credibility, expertise, and influence.	I do extra research and consider all the possibilities when coordinating new projects.
After delivering the initial outline of new objectives, I don't get involved in the implementation of daily procedures and tasks associated with the goal.	I learn from my mistakes and I help others to do the same.	I work to build strong relationships both interdepartmentally as well as intradepartmentally.
I offer generalized expectations but don't bother to offer further guidance.	I effectively influence the actions and opinions of others.	I am considered by others to be a person of high personal and professional integrity.
Many employees bypass me entirely because I am not seen as an expert or as trustworthy.	I recognize potential in others and I give recognition when appropriate.	I actively recruit the best in the field and work to create an environment in which each person thrives.
I am often unavailable and have a short fuse, especially when informed about problems.	I define team roles and responsibilities and delegate opportunities for achievement.	I encourage all employees to explore their potential and hold monthly goal-setting conversations.
The only time I offer feedback is at annual performance reviews.	I communicate a sense of urgency.	I invite open dialog by interacting and soliciting feedback on a weekly basis.
I rarely enforce disciplinary action but I do rely on threats and fear tactics when I feel forced to provide motivators.	I provide subordinates with regular feedback on results achieved.	I stay informed and address issues immediately and I am proactive about corrective measures for discipline and performance problems.
	I provide recognition for a job well done.	I invite feedback about my own managing skills in order to ensure my effectiveness.
	I recognize the importance of taking corrective action when employee performance warrants it and initiate that action when necessary.	

WORD PICTURES IN ACTION: CAESARS ENTERTAINMENT CORPORATION

Caesars Entertainment Corporation is the largest casino entertainment company in the world. It owns and operates casinos, hotels, and golf courses under brand names that include Harrah's, Caesars Palace, Bally's, Paris, Rio, Flamingo, and the Imperial Palace. It has more than 60,000 employees and is committed to hiring for—and teaching—attitude. Even in the midst of a global recession, Caesars Entertainment continues to reach new customer satisfaction benchmarks.

Caesars Entertainment is a great organization, so I was delighted to head to Las Vegas when Terry Byrnes, Vice President of Total Service, gave me a call. (Plus, hanging out in Las Vegas at Caesars Palace is not exactly a hardship.) Terry is well known and respected in the service world and has developed numerous innovations for delivering sophisticated customer service.

Terry and his team had assessed untold hours of mystery shopper video and knew exactly where service breakdowns occurred. They had also diagnosed their customers' psychological state at every stage of the visit—from entry to exit, and every game, show, meal, and rest in between. Customer satisfaction metrics and predictions are world class; the team knows precisely how much more, or less, customers will spend depending on how delighted they were on their last trip.

On top of all that, Terry had assessed 30 properties around the country and knew exactly what separated high performers from everyone else. He knew that the organization's Brown Shorts were built around a concept of ownership. High performers across the Caesars properties take ownership for delighting customers (and anticipating their preferences and needs); knowing the answers to the most important guest questions (where everything is and what's going on); initiating interactions; and delivering service with quality, accuracy, and speed.

Terry had revolutionized the science of total service. Now he wanted an equally innovative technique for embedding these practices more thoroughly in the Caesars culture. He immediately loved the science behind Word Pictures. His first thought was that this was a great way to stamp out some of the behaviors that were undermining performance. Because as good as Caesars is, there are 60,000 employees out there, and some of them are not going to be performing at the highest levels. When that happens, guest satisfaction drops, which in turn means suboptimizing financial performance. According to Caesars' CEO, a spending increase of only $5 per guest (about as much as a fancy coffee) in its regional markets would add nearly $50 million to its bottom line. (Those regional markets do not include Las Vegas or Atlantic City, so this is just a fraction of the total possible opportunity.)

So here's what happened. Caesars' research, analytics, intuitions, and experience were distilled into the following five key Brown Shorts characteristics: initiate, know, delight, deliver, and own. Then Word Pictures descriptions were created for each characteristic. I can't share all of them with you—after all, what happens in Vegas, stays in Vegas—but I can show you some examples.

As a side note here, I need to mention that Word Pictures, like Brown Shorts, are meant to be customized to fit your culture. That's a good bit of what we do at Leadership IQ. So at Caesars, Needs Work and Great Work are now called Never Acceptable and Role Model—different words, same system.

Here are a few Word Picture examples from the know and own categories:

Role model: When you don't know, thank your guests for their patience and maintain ownership until someone can help.

Never acceptable: Guess or give out information of doubtful accuracy. Send the customers away without ensuring a suitable answer.

Role model: Report new or difficult questions to your supervisor so he or she can investigate and get back to you.

Never acceptable: Fail to report new or difficult questions.

Role model: Make it easy for your guests to get the answer by knowing the hours, prices, times, and locations of key property features and events.

Never acceptable: Start your shift unprepared to answer the most common and important guest questions.

Role model: Be optimistic and speak positively about guests, coworkers, management, and the company. Offer helpful suggestions.

Never acceptable: Complain, or speak negatively without offering legitimate suggestions for improvement.

Now, having Word Pictures is great, but we do have to actually use them. So it was determined that these lessons in high performance would be taught via monthly learning activities. Each month, supervisors were trained in a short buzz session—

five minutes dedicated to building an awareness of the Word Pictures that reflected that month's chosen topic (for example, know or own).

Supervisors were then sent out into the field and directed to find appropriate real-life learning opportunities that addressed that month's topic and to deliver an individual 12-minute coaching session to each employee using those Word Pictures. Terry didn't sit employees in a class and pound initiate, know, delight, deliver, and own into their heads for eight hours. No, Caesars took its Word Pictures out of the classroom and onto the floor and used them as live coaching tools.

This only works because of Word Pictures' Behavioral Specificity and positive/negative example learning design. Abstract teaching or only using positive examples, like most traditional workplace training programs, just don't work for this type of on-the-floor training.

Another bonus made possible by the design of Word Pictures was an employee self-evaluation. You see, this isn't just about managers teaching employees; it's about employees actually learning. So every month, coupled with the one-on-one coaching sessions, employees use Word Pictures to assess their own performance. This develops employees' critical self-awareness and, because of the Behavioral Specificity and learning design of Word Pictures, they immediately see where they should focus their personal improvement efforts.

Now, this is Caesars. So there are some sophisticated incentives tied to this. There's a tracking system for accountability, there are chips awarded to reinforce behaviors, and more. But fundamentally, Terry will tell you this whole program is about changing what, where, and how employees learn about delivering excellent service.

Terry's not just a remarkably innovative service expert; he's also one heck of a training innovator. This cultural change does not require trainers, space, or formal scheduling. Simply put, there are no additional labor costs. And in a truly radical paradigm shift, employee development will eventually be owned by operations, not HR.

For 22 minutes per employee per month, for six months, Caesars will get the following:

- Team members known as the most willing to serve found anywhere
- In response to customer questions, the first employee asked provides a compelling answer
- The skill and attitude of employees becoming the most compelling reason to visit
- Maximized fulfillment, quality, and efficiency through individual performance
- Extremely well-served guests because team members love their work

As I mentioned, Caesars has sophisticated and proprietary models that show exactly how much more customers spend when they're delighted. As I told you earlier, even an extra $5 spent per customer at the regional properties (not including Las Vegas or Atlantic City) would add nearly $50 million to Caesars' bottom line. Since we're "in" Las Vegas, let me put all my cards on the table: I'm not allowed to divulge what the total payoff will be. But I can say that a few Brown Shorts and Word Pictures, along with an innovative training approach, are going to earn Caesars a lot more cash than the typical marketing campaign or cost-cutting effort. And that's no gamble. (Ba-dum-dum.)

A FINAL THOUGHT

Leadership IQ has an entire consulting practice devoted to helping organizations develop Word Pictures. And while we're aided by a big library of preexisting Word Pictures, it's important for our clients to remember that their Word Pictures need to reflect their unique culture. It may seem as though it would be quicker to buy our library and call it a day, but that approach doesn't generate deep buy-in from employees—the people who will actually be living in the organization every day. So, by all means, use the examples in this chapter as a starting point and a teaching tool. But then, work hard to make your Word Pictures reflect your unique culture.

For free downloadable resources including the latest research, discussion guides, and forms please visit www.leadershipiq.com/hiring.

Conclusion

As I said at the beginning, this book is about attitude. It's about how to select for attitude, interview for attitude, recruit for attitude, assess peoples' attitude, and even teach attitude. Because whether you're hiring your next hourly employee, your next CEO, or something in between, attitude will likely be the issue that determines success or failure.

Brown Shorts and Word Pictures are big concepts. But if you break them down, step-by-step, you'll find that you can succeed fairly quickly. As a reminder of everything we covered (and I always like a quick recap of what I just learned), here's a distillation of the big points in this book:

- **The attitude that works for your organization is unique (Chapter 1).** Your organization's culture, and the attitudes required to succeed in that culture, are unique. This means that the "right" attitudes that define a high performer will vary from culture to culture. Find your Brown Shorts and you will find your secret source of competitive advantage.
- **Standard interview questions don't assess attitude (Chapter 2).** Most interview questions are useless for

assessing attitude, and some can even put your company at legal risk. So eliminate the four types of common interview questions that undermine your ability to assess attitude.

- **A few simple questions will reveal if someone's attitude is right for you (Chapter 3).** The only interview questions that reveal whether or not a candidate is a match for your organization are those targeting the attitudes that matter most to your organization. So create your Brown Shorts Interview Questions and start learning whether candidates have the right attitude for your organization.

- **There's an answer key that will grade a candidate's attitude (Chapter 4).** What's the point of asking a question if you have no idea how to grade the answer? Build your Brown Shorts Answer Guidelines and never again hire on a hunch.

- **The grammar that people use (pronouns, verbs, and adverbs) predicts whether they're a good or bad fit (Chapter 5).** You've got great questions, and you've got an answer key, so use them to consistently evaluate your candidates. Listen to the words people use and how they use them—word choices reveal tremendous amounts about attitude.

- **The way most companies recruit chases away the best people (Chapter 6).** The talent pipelines at most organizations are filled with everyone but the right people for that organization. So use your Brown Shorts and the recruiting formula to fill your talent pool with the people right for you. And avoid the people who aren't right for you.

- **Hiring for Attitude will make your current employees even better (Chapter 7).** You want to hire for attitude, but the quest for high performance shouldn't stop there. You also want to develop more high performers from the folks you already have working in your company. So use Word Pictures and propagate the right attitudes throughout the whole organization.

Hiring for Attitude gives you a new set of tools for making great hiring choices. And when you're ready for the next level, you can become certified in Hiring for Attitude. It's an online or live program that will give you (and every hiring manager in your organization) an advanced skill set for selecting stars with great attitudes. Plus—it looks good on a résumé should you ever find yourself on the other side of the hiring equation.

Stay in touch with us and get all the latest research updates (and learn more about certification) at www.leadershipiq.com/ hiring.

Index

About the Author

Mark Murphy is the founder and CEO of Leadership IQ (www.leadershipiq.com). Since its inception, Leadership IQ has become a top-rated provider of goal-setting training, leadership training, employee surveys and e-learning. As the force behind some of the largest leadership studies ever conducted, Leadership IQ's programs have yielded remarkable results for such organizations as Microsoft, IBM, MasterCard, Merck, MD Anderson Cancer Center, FirstEnergy, Volkswagen, and Johns Hopkins. Murphy's cutting-edge leadership techniques and research have been featured in *Fortune, Forbes, Business-Week, U.S. News & World Report*, the *Washington Post*, and hundreds more periodicals. He was featured on a "CBS News Sunday Morning" special report on slackers in the workplace as well as being featured on ABC's "20/20." He has also made several appearances on "Fox Business News."

Murphy also authored the international bestsellers *Hundred Percenters: Challenge Your People to Give It Their All and They'll Give You Even More* and *HARD Goals: The Secret to Getting from Where You Are to Where You Want to Be.*

A former turnaround advisor, Murphy guided more than a hundred organizations from precarious financial situations to record-setting levels of prosperity. For these and other accomplishments, Murphy was a three-time nominee for Modern Healthcare's Most Powerful People in Healthcare Award, joining a list of 300 luminaries including George W. Bush and Hillary Clinton. Only 15 consultants had ever been nominated to this list. He was also awarded the Healthcare Financial Management Association's Helen Yerger Award for Best Research.

A seasoned public speaker, Murphy has illuminated audiences for hundreds of groups and lectured at the Harvard Business School, Yale University, the University of Rochester, and the University of Florida.

For free downloadable resources about this book, please visit www.leadershipiq.com/hiring